WOMEN LIKE ME

Whispers of Warriors: Women Who Refused to Stay Broken

JULIE FAIRHURST

Tuns Feb 22%

YOU ARE A STRONG and Beautiful women Warrior women who reFuses to stay Broken
Always Remember This —A Friend in need is a friend in Deed...

To Lynda my Friend to the End
we may Be Broke But...
Never Broken (LoL)
my heart goes out to you
during this time of healing
your Bones

Healing OF... your ♡ heart and, surrounded By Love ♡ ALWAYS...
Knowing your NEVER ALONE...!!!☆☆☆

" not Above you
not Below you,
But right Beside you"
NEVER ALONE

Love ya sister friend
call me or text For
Anything you might need
and I'll be there For you
Winter spring summer or Fall
Cause All you have to do is call

♪ and I'll be there ♪ ♪ cause you've Got a Friend ♪

Compiled by Julie Fairhurst
Copyright Julie Fairhurst 2023 – Rock Star Publishing
Paperback Edition: ISBN: 978-1-990639-17-3
Interior & Cover Design by STOKE Publishing

The authors of this book do not dispense medical advice or prescribe the use of any technique as a form of treatment for physical, emotional, or medical problems without a physician's advice, either directly or indirectly. The authors intend to provide general information to individuals taking positive steps in their lives for emotional and spiritual well-being. If you use any information in this book for yourself, which is your constitutional right, the authors and the publishers assume no responsibility for your actions.

At times, some readers may be triggered by a women's story. Should you need to speak with someone, there are many crisis lines, counselors, and doctors that you can reach out to. Find someone who can lend a kind ear to listen to you. That can be a friend, parent, spouse, or anyone you trust. Your local community services may have telephone numbers to assist you.

Contents

Introduction   vii

Part I

Whispers of Warriors

1. Escaping A Convicted Killer   3
2. A Single Mom's Un-Hypnotizing Journey   23
3. The Will To Live   29
4. The Desire To Do Better   51
5. Will This Pain Ever Go Away?   61
6. My Mother Who Couldn't Love Me   73
7. Diamonds Are Created Under Pressure   85
8. Tears Into Triumph   93
9. A Shattered Heart   105
10. Heather's Tree   117

Part II

Meet the Contributors

The Warriors Behind The Whispers

KAY BOHEMIER   133
JILL FISCHER   135
KATHERINE WELLS   137
LISA HUPPEE   139
HANNAH THURIER   143
JOANNE SMITH   145
CALLIE JENSEN   147
JULIA HIK   149
NICOLE SARAH DUPONT-SCOTT   151
HEATHER O'REILLY   153

Part III

About Women Like Me

Women Like Me Community   157
Women Like Me Book Series   161
Julie Fairhurst   165
Read More From Julie Fairhurst   171

"I am a warrior in the time of women warriors; the longing for justice is the sword I carry."

Sonia Johnson

Introduction

Women's stories have been overshadowed, overlooked, or erased throughout history. However, despite these challenges, remarkable women have defied and spoken out. Their voices, no matter how small or unheard, have added to the rich fabric of humanity and paved the way for future generations.

I'm a woman like me, a whispering warrior. I am not always loud, but my voice matters. I may be quiet, but I speak volumes with my presence. I am a woman like me, a whispered warrior. I don't always make a lot of noise, but what I have to say is important, and others listen. I may be gentle, but my words hold power.

This remarkable collection honors the inspiring stories of ten individuals who have demonstrated incredible strength and resilience in the face of adversity. Their stories serve as a powerful reminder that the human spirit can triumph despite seemingly insurmountable challenges.

Through their stories, we are reminded of the incredible strength that lies within each of us and of the healing that can occur when we share our struggles and triumphs with others.

Note · Lynda I Bought this For you as the cover and title spoke to me For you and In couriousity read it so I could Fully understand my Gift to you...

Each story in this remarkable book holds a profound message, a cherished wisdom passed down through the generations. These inspiring women have endured hardships that many of us can only imagine, such as abuse, neglect, and heartbreak.

Yet, they have emerged stronger, more resilient, and determined to reshape their paths.

Their stories serve as powerful reminders of what is possible when we have the courage to rise above adversity and embrace the power of transformation. Let their triumphs be your guide, and let their unwavering spirits ignite a fire within you to overcome any challenge that comes your way.

The aim of Women Like Me is more than just retelling suffering. It's using words to create a vivid image of optimism. It's discovering resilience in openness, meaning in hardship, and speaking up in the midst of hopelessness. As you explore the chapters, you're not just absorbing their words but accompanying heroes on their journey.

If you're seeking comfort, guidance, or a sense of belonging, take heart in knowing that you're not alone. This book serves as a heartfelt connection, a bridge between souls. For those who feel shattered, let these warrior's words be a gentle whisper: You possess the power to mend, the bravery to speak up, and the ability to create a different storyline.

Remember, your struggles do not define you, but the resilience and strength you exhibit in overcoming them. Welcome to a symphony of resilience. These stories, shared by remarkable women, are a testament to the power of refusing to accept defeat.

As you read, allow their stories to resonate within your soul, for they echo all our struggles and triumphs. Their words hold the power to inspire and empower you, guiding you toward a new chapter filled with hope, healing, and endless possibilities.

Embrace this journey of self-discovery, and let their courage be your driving force, for within you lie the strength and determination to overcome any obstacle and write your very own triumphant story.

JULIE FAIRHURST

FOUNDER OF WOMEN LIKE ME

continued and little did I know I was meant to read this also for me which concludes my desire to continue my Gatherings of women empowering Women club in a group I've named.

NEVER ALONE

so much summer time plans here in my Back yard to come. The list is long... so Glad you are a part of this club.

"You have never been and you won't ever be wrong for choosing yourself!

Read that again …"

Samiha Totanji

PART I
Whispers of Warriors

Lynda
Warrior women

ONE

Escaping A Convicted Killer

ONE SURVIVOR'S HARROWING TALE

"If your strong enough to stay, your strong enough to leave."
Kay Bohemier

After the second blow to my head from his fist, I felt a numb, hot sensation throughout my body. I felt like I began to float and could not feel any more pain. Was this how it felt when you were about to die? Was I going to die on the side of the road in my car? I didn't even have a chance to fight back. The punches came out of nowhere. The last thing I remember him saying to me was, "I'm going to kill you."

When I came to, there was blood everywhere. I was covered in blood. I realized I was pulled out of my car, dragged, and stuffed into the passenger seat. He was now driving. I screamed over and over, "Please don't let me die," "Please don't let me die," "Take me to the hospital". Instead, I was held against my will and kidnapped as I was bleeding to death.

He drove miles and miles until he ran the car out of gas. I remember him pulling into a gas station, but everything seemed in slow motion. I was suffering from a serious head injury. I was so weak I could hardly move. My body felt numb, and my thinking was all scrambled.

The minute I had as he stood outside the vehicle, I managed to take a picture of myself with my cell phone to see why I was covered in blood. I was in shock. I could see my earlobe was detached from my head, and it looked like my eye was missing. I knew I would die that night if I didn't figure out how to get help.

I knew the only way was to send that picture to my friend in Canada. I had seconds to accomplish this, and I knew calling 911 would have gotten me killed if my attacker had seen me on my cell.

My name is Kay, and this is a story about surviving severe domestic abuse at the hands of a convicted murderer. Looking back, I had a pattern of helping those struggling, whether taking kids to my home or digging through my purse holding up traffic to give money to the homeless standing in the street. I'm 52 years old, a mother of five beautiful grown children, born and raised in Winnipeg, Manitoba, Canada.

Life was routine once my kids were grown and moved out. Woke up, went to work, came home, and went to bed. I had nice, pretty things, my own home, and my dream car. I considered myself educated with a degree in Local Government and certified as a City Manager, but I also got bored quickly once I mastered a role. I decided to get my professional driver's license, and I moved on to working in the oilfields. I'm a go-getter and always look at the glass as half full instead of half empty. Problems in my life were always tackled as challenges, never problems.

As I reflect on my childhood, well, you could say it wasn't very stable. I was given up for adoption at the age of one and a half years old, and the family who adopted me were very abusive. Throughout my younger years, I was physically and sexually abused by my father, and while dealing with that, my brother died at the age of nine. Eventually, I put myself into foster care at the age of 15. By the time I was 18 years old, I was already working at a prestigious law firm completely on my own. Eventually, I married and had my beautiful children, but it ended after 14 years of marriage.

At this time in my life, the "wanting to help somebody" kicked in, and all it took was watching a Netflix documentary. "How prisoners in segregation are treated." I knew nothing about criminal life or the prison system, and after understanding how some prisoners are treated less than human, it upset me. Yes, crime does the time, but why is there a need to treat them less than human? I felt an urge to act, to make a difference in a life suffering through that. Perhaps I felt the need to help because I desperately needed that help growing up, but it never came.

The next morning, I Googled how to write a prisoner, and to my astonishment, a website that connected people to prisoners popped up. I read page after page of inmate stories and eventually chose three inmates to write to. Two inmates were in the USA, and one inmate was from Canada.

My intentions to write were purely coming from a good place. Encouraging them to do better, not allowing the crime to define who they were but believing that one could change, and finally showing them that one person cared to treat them like human beings. I was shocked when one of those inmates wrote back. His name was John Gaddy. John's letter contained brilliant penmanship, and the words filled the paper with excitement, hopes, and dreams.

This man spoke about how he was rehabilitated and wanted to be remembered for the good he would do in his community. He had worked diligently to finish schooling in prison and continued to take any offered courses that became available to him. He was very proud of what he had accomplished, and he thanked me continuously throughout his letter that I was kind enough to show compassion and understanding.

John was in prison for a manslaughter conviction. He was 25 when he was arrested. The first question I asked him was why did you do it? He replied, "It was self-defense," and that his neighbor had attacked him with a knife. John went on to say that he was only protecting himself and that he felt horrible about what had happened.

Three little words I said to John changed my life forever. Those words were, "**I believe you.**"

Our relationship continued to progress through letters and then, eventually, phone calls. I believe we really got to know each other. One of his dreams was to open a fitness center that served healthy food, and together, we made a business plan and even designed business cards. Our relationship continued to grow, and we became as close as two people could be without any physical contact.

There became a point in our friendship that turned into something more, and John asked me to come to see him at the prison. Despite warnings from everybody in my life, I believed in my soul it was a journey I was meant to take. Some called it stupid, and some called it dangerous. I called it compassion for another human being. He was paying for his crime with his freedom. What more could he do? I have never judged, and I felt as though we weren't in his shoes, none of us were there that horrible night, and John insisted it was in self-defense.

I traveled to see him for a one-hour non-contact visit, leaving from central Canada to take the journey to the prison in North Carolina, more than 2,500 miles away. The visit was incredible. It felt like we had known each other for a lifetime. As time went on, a plan ensued to which I would pick him up on his release date and spend six months in the USA.

I nervously waited for him in the prison parking lot on the day of his release. I felt like a teenager, so excited to hug, touch, and kiss him. As I gazed at the front doors to the prison, I saw a man walk through the doors wearing the clothes I had just dropped off to the prison guard. There he was!!!!! Free!!!!!! He was holding freshly picked flowers with the biggest smile I've ever seen. He immediately picked me up and spun me around. To my surprise, he was crying. We embraced each other so tightly that it felt like time stood still. Watching him experience freedom was truly something spectacular. It sure put into perspective how I took my freedom for granted. John served nine years of his 11-year sentence, so his freedom didn't come without strings attached.

John was placed on supervised probation established by the North Carolina Post-Release Supervision and Parole Commission. This meant if John violated any of his probation conditions, he could be sent back to prison to serve his remaining maximum sentence imposed term of 11 years. Some of John's conditions were not to use, possess, or control any illegal drug or controlled substances; not possess a firearm, destructive device, or other dangerous weapon unless granted written permission by his probation officer; not leave his county of residence unless permission was granted; and not commit another crime while on Post-Release.

Even with all the conditions, John and I spent every moment together. He and I went on long car rides exploring, even though he was very limited in where he could go. We spent time at the park a lot talking and building our relationship. I helped John get established outside of prison. We made his resume. I taught him how to apply for jobs online. I took him to get a cell phone, helped him study to get his driver's license, and showed him how to use online banking.

John and I easily related as we shared a similar childhood. John's mother abandoned him when he was very little, and my mother gave me up for adoption. John alleged his father was extremely abusive to him growing up, and my father was also very abusive to me. We knew each other so well that we could finish each other's sentences, and we both had the ability to know what each of us needed without asking. John and I were putting into action what we set out to do in the hundreds and hundreds of letters and phone calls we had while he was in prison.

John and I resided at his grandmother's, but he was required to find his own place as soon as he could, as this was only temporary. We researched what resources he could get to help with finding his own place, but it became evident that convicted felons are treated differently. Housing is almost impossible to find, and most employers do background checks, but despite the hurdles John got hired as a pipe layer for a construction company in the county where he resided, and I obtained housing for him by putting the lease in my name.

By October, which was one month after his release from prison, I could clearly see John's temper surface. It went from being irritated over small things to downright screaming confrontations. I finally questioned him about what was wrong, and he would say things like, "Nothing, what the f**k is wrong with you."

On top of the outbursts, John would say out of the blue, "Can you see the demons"? "They are coming to get me, Kay?" I would ask him why he thought that, and John said, "Because I sold my soul to the devil." There were times while watching TV, I would observe John staring down the hallway, cowering on the couch, scarily saying to me, "Kay, can you see the Grimm reaper"?

He would cower under the blankets, sobbing for them to leave him alone. I would stay up with him for hours consoling him, ensuring him that there weren't demons in the bedroom, and would rub his back till he would fall asleep. These hallucinations were becoming a daily occurrence, and I started to feel uneasy with the situation. What on earth was going on with him?

John left home very young because of the alleged abuse, and he began associating with gang members. Eventually, John took comfort in what the gang stood for. The "we got each other's backs" and "we are a family" mentality didn't take long for John to go through the gang initiation and become part of that family.

John worked his way up in his gang over a period of years and eventually earned a high-rank status. High-rank status gave John the authority to call shots to lower members. Were the demons of his conscience coming back to haunt him over the horrible crimes he committed while in the gang? Unknown to me, his dirty little secrets would rear their ugly heads days before I escaped.

By November, John had already physically attacked me twice. I explained it away by saying he was under a lot of pressure, and I thought perhaps he was a little institutionalized, being in prison for nine years. According to John, his affiliation with the gang had ended, and all that was left to do was gain approval from three members to become inactive members. The plan was I would drive him to the gang clubhouse, and he would get initiated out by beating out by three high-rank members…. that day never came.

Most of our fights were my concerns with him beginning to contact old gang friends who were drug users. I was so confused. John made it crystal clear to me several times that he was leaving his old ways in the past, not to mention it's a violation of his probation, so why on earth was he willing to jeopardize all we had accomplished, not to mention his freedom by digging up old skeletons from the past. Of course, when I brought that subject up, he went from zero to 100, which looked like the veins in his neck bulging, and he would inflate himself by pumping up his chest muscles.

One conversation took place in the bedroom. We were standing by the bedroom door. The next thing I knew, he wound up and slapped me across the face so violently I fell to the bed. I was dazed. John then got on top of me, put his hands around my neck, and started strangling me. The feeling of having your oxygen completely cut off is hard to describe. You have been stripped of all control, and the oxygen that keeps you alive has been taken away. You slowly feel weak, and keeping your eyes open is hard as you start slipping into a daze of unconsciousness. For some reason, John let go. I gasped for air as my body lay on the bed, tingling.

The next morning, I awoke to a ringing ear, a swollen and bruised neck, and severe issues swallowing. John entered my room sobbing. He got on his knees and placed his head on my lap, begging me to forgive him. John was a master manipulator. He could twist and turn reasons for his behavior in any situation, and of course, he played on my emotions. I felt sorry for him and always forgave him.

As time progressed, John's whole demeanor changed. He was now wearing colored bandanas, he became more secretive, and his short temper was pretty much a daily occurrence. Strange, least desirable people were starting to come to the house packed with guns who were introduced to me as old friends.

Early December, I was again attacked by John, this time over a conversation about blowing off his curfew at 9 p.m. In this fight, he threw me against the bedroom window, threw me to the bed, and pinned me there. I screamed and begged for him to get off me, but not until I vomited did, he let me go. He cried right after it happened and promised to seek counseling for his bad temper. John said he would never hurt somebody he loved and was truly sorry.

I could see that John's mental state was not well. There was something wrong, but I was determined to be there for him because I loved him. On the good days, John told me I was the best thing that ever happened to him and that he loved me more than he could ever put into words.

As the relationship progressed into December, we got a Christmas tree and decorated the house. We spent evenings playing Scrabble together and working on our relationship.

By December, John's mental state worsened. His hallucinations were becoming more frequent, and his angry outbursts towards me were increasing. John would say things like I can't communicate like a normal human being, and no wonder my last husband divorced me.

Again, in December, John was angry again, and I didn't understand why. He became enraged, saying that I was not supportive enough, and said he was suicidal. I told him if he felt suicidal, I would call 911. John burst out screaming that if I threatened to call 911, he was going to beat me to god damm hell, and twice in that fight, he said he would kill me and himself, and we would land up on ABC news. I should have left him by this time as the danger flags were screaming.

However, I believed John would get help, and I was determined to see it through.

John got approval from his probation officer to head up to the Appalachian mountains to camp over Christmas. Those two days were awesome. John and I loaded up a tent and everything we needed and went hiking off-trail in the backcountry. We set up a tent on Christmas Eve, made a bonfire, and enjoyed each other. It was a very special moment for me. John and I worked amazingly well as a team. We both had the same ideas, so there was never any fighting when it came to teamwork.

One day, John got home from work and asked me to open the trunk. To my amazement, there was a ring in a box open with a poem he had written to me. He asked me to marry him. I was crying and so happy, and of course, I said yes. He told me that I was the best thing that ever happened to him, and he could not see his life without me. We wanted to be married the weekend of Valentine's Day. So, we settled on February 16th. During this time, I explained away the abuse and convinced myself John would be getting counseling and that he truly didn't mean to hurt me.

Things moved into January, and the relationship seemed to be a bit better. John's hallucinations continued, though, and so did his impulsive behaviors. John would get periods of severe depression followed by heightened levels of hypermania where he would make horrible decisions. I finally convinced John to go to see a mental health counselor. John refused to go unless I went with him. I told John I would do anything to support him and go with him because that's what you do when you love someone.

We met with a professional mental health counselor, where she assessed John. He was diagnosed with Bipolar 1 with manic episodes and hallucinations. He was prescribed medication. John outright refused to take his medication and said he would control his mood independently. This was becoming very problematic as his mood was up and down, and his verbal abuse was worsening. He would call me a dirty cunt, or a stinking ass hoe, he would belittle me by calling me stupid, and he would say I was fat, but he could see potential if I just got off my lazy ass and worked out with him.

John was fired from his job in January 2020 as his behavior was erratic. One of the last days he worked, he never made it to work; he sat on the side of the road all day and didn't call me or anybody. He claimed he ran out of gas. His erratic behavior was becoming worse.

John stressed that he could not pay rent, utilities, or any financial responsibilities. I decided to sell my car in February to help him with the bills. We still had John's car.

We were married by a Pastor at Friendly Baptist Church. This was the same church John and I attended together and the same church John attended his men's group. John and I wrote our own vows. John's family and my children attended the service through Skype. John's dad walked me down the aisle, and John's sister Linda was my maid of honor. Linda is John's only sibling. Linda is much older than John and did her best growing up to care for her little brother. My relationship with Linda became very close; she played a vital role later.

Our reception was held at John's Grandma's. We had a wedding cake and a full buffet-style meal. It was one of the happiest days of my life. I loved John so much and believed I had married my forever man. We took our own pictures with cell phones, and the church made a video CD of the marriage ceremony.

By March, John was a different person. He would stand in the bathroom for hours and hours, picking at his face. He would go 2-3 days with no sleep. One night, I was asleep and woke to John standing at the foot of our bed, wearing a black balaclava and he was holding a machete. I jumped up on the bed, screaming at him, "John, John, what are you doing?" It was like he was in a trance. I literally stood up on the bed and launched myself passed him straight through the front door of the house in my pajamas barefoot and hid behind a gas station at the end of our street and stayed hidden for hours, eventually returning to an apologetic John, who said he was just playing around.

Also, in March, I was watching TV on the couch. It was early morning, around 1:00 a.m. John demanded I walk with him into the woods outback our home. He was holding a machete. I asked him why, and he said he was going to look for flowers. I was scared to death and told him I did not want to go. He became upset and said you are going and was becoming very angry. I knew I had to go; he was holding the machete and becoming belligerent.

The pit of my soul was screaming he's going to kill you. The feeling of having all your control taken away truly puts a person in a state of pure panic and a feeling of helplessness. I got off the couch, my legs shaking, and I remember my heart beating so fast I felt like I was having an out-of-body experience. My mind was seeing the machete and hearing his voice, yet I felt as though my spirit had checked out.

My mind was racing as I slowly walked towards the house's back door, John following behind, holding that machete. I remember talking to God in that moment I opened the door and left the house. "God, please don't let me die. Please help me, PLEASE."

I slowly started the descent down the six steps of our deck, which took us to the driveway. John fixated on me from behind. When we reached the driveway, John told me to grab and push the wheel barrel, which was sitting just outside the garage door. I asked him why, and John replied, it's for the flowers I'm going to cut. In my mind, I thought, this is it. He's going to kill me, put my body in that wheel barrel, and bury me out back. I was the flowers he was going to cut up.

As soon as we came upon the edge of the woods, John walked right past me and started violently chopping the tall grass, mumbling words I could not understand. I let go of the wheel barrel and stood frozen, watching. Could I run? No. John could have easily outrun me. Could anybody see me from the road? No. It was too dark. The only way out was to talk myself out. I desperately held back my tears and blurted out, "John, I really have to go to the bathroom." John ignored me, continuously slamming the machete into the tall grass.

He was acting like someone from a different world, speaking some kind of language I could not understand. I said it again, but I asserted my voice with sternness this time. "John, I really need to go to the bathroom." The swathing stopped. John lifted his head, walked over to me face to face, and said, "Shut the f***k up, GO." I turned around and ran to the house, locked myself in the bathroom, and tried to compose myself. We never returned to the woods that night, nor did we ever speak about it after that night. As far as I know, the wheel barrel remained at the edge of those woods, never to be moved again.

Although I kept the abuse a secret from everyone except Linda, I did call John's probation officer and explained my serious concerns about his mental state. Unfortunately, this was a waste of my time as no help was given, so I knew I better devise a plan for John. Linda and I spoke daily to figure out what we could do to get John's help.

After pleading with John to go to the emergency room, he finally agreed to be assessed by a doctor as he was back to feeling suicidal. I took him to the hospital, and they treated him as being suicidal. Although John went voluntarily, the hospital decided to change it to involuntary once they assessed him. They placed two security guards at his hospital room door. John was belligerent again, swearing at hospital staff and punching a hole in the wall of his room. John refused to cooperate unless the hospital allowed me to remain in the room with him.

I slept on the hard concrete floor beside John's hospital bed. I spoke with the on-call psychiatrist and told them all about his bizarre behavior, hallucinations, and obsessive-compulsive behavior. They admitted John and kept him for two days. He was released with prescriptions to help him with his anxiety. We honestly accomplished nothing as John absolutely refused to take the medication. It was clear to me at this point that John's compromised state was not going to change without the medication, and I knew that my physical and mental state was in jeopardy. I was becoming afraid of my husband's unpredictable, severe anger outbursts. His hallucinations were so severe that it was affecting his decision-making abilities.

As the days went by, refusing to take his medication, John was deteriorating quickly, and he refused any treatment at all. The situation was beyond volatile and very dangerous. I decided to go to the court house in the county where we resided to see a magistrate and asked for the court to issue an involuntary order to take John back to hospital.

Police picked John up and brought him to the Hospital. They ran tests, and I found out he tested positive for methamphetamine (meth). It wasn't until this point that I found out John had a drug problem and was hiding it from me.

John was transferred to Charlotte Hospital for further assessment. He begged me to take him out of the hospital. He cried and cried, and when I said no, John took me off as his beneficiary to speak with doctors. During this time, Linda expressed serious concern for my safety and suggested at stay in a women's shelter. She knew her brother was angry with me for having him committed.

My heart hurt so bad for him that I had him committed. It was that, or he was going to land up right back in prison or hurt me again. I did this because I wanted him to get better. I wanted the loving man who was my whole life back. I wanted my husband back, the man who promised to protect me, take care of me, and love me, not beat on me, mentally attack me, and make me afraid to be in the same house as him.

John was released about two weeks after he was committed. I had gotten him enrolled in counseling again and even had him signed up to have a specialist come to the house to see him because of his anxiety. I thought John was attending all his sessions, and when I went to check in with his counselor, I found out that he had blown off almost a month's worth of appointments. John's counselor was afraid for my safety and felt I was in danger, and so was John's sister Linda.

John was harboring ill feelings towards me for having him committed, and his mental abuse became beyond words can describe. Nothing I did was right. He said I didn't love him right. I didn't support him right. He said I was just a white trash gutter girl who was no longer his ride or die. He said that I had a stinking ass pussy, and I was a cunt. Being in the house with John was like walking on pins and needles. You never knew what would set him off. Simple features of kindness, such as asking him if he would like a coffee, would put John into a fit of rage, and if I tried to walk away, he would threaten to beat me.

I finally came to accept that John was not going to change and came to the realization that if I didn't get out, John would eventually kill me. I started to plan to escape. This plan was going to be difficult as I needed to get back to Canada. I had no money and did not have a car. I could not work in the USA without a work permit. I started making secret calls to a shelter in Canada to help me with a plan and was secretly speaking to a counselor in North Carolina.

While out with John's car, I had come home early and could see the front door to our house was open. Once inside, I noticed all my pictures of John and me were stuffed under the bed, with no sign of John anywhere. I started back to the car looking for him and eventually found him walking a few blocks from our house with a girl walking the opposite way.

Once home, I questioned him about the girl and the fact that all the pictures were hidden under the bed, and of course, he told me I was crazy and making things up in my head. John denied cheating on me. One of my last conversations with John was about a tattoo he proudly wore on his arm. After asking him for months about it, John, out of the blue, said, "It represents how many people I've killed." I asked John how many people there were, and he replied, "Nine."

Two days later, on May 16th Linda called me and asked about my escape plan. I shared with her what John had told me about committing nine murders and asked her if she thought it could be true. Linda never answered my question. She replied, "Kay, you have no more time left for plans, you need to leave the house today and never look back, my brother is going to kill you". I listened. I promised I would leave that day. The only way out was to take our car, as I sold mine. John, of course, was with me all day. It wasn't until later that evening, when he went to take a shower, that I had any opportunity.

He had placed his cell phone and wallet on the couch in the sitting room just outside the bathroom, and of course, he was showering with the door open. My heart was pounding, and I was shaking, but I mustered up the courage to tiptoe to the couch. I very carefully and quietly picked up the car keys and his cell phone, placed both inside my shirt, and emptied his wallet with the money he had inside. The plan after his shower was to have a bonfire, so I said aloud, "John, I'm going to go out back and collect firewood," John replied, "Okay."

I had no time to pack anything other than what I was wearing and what was in my purse. I walked out the back door, got into the car and drove away. That moment felt surreal. It felt like a dream, physically was driving the car but in shock, I got out this time. This was the eighth time I left, but this time, not only did I get caught, but this time, I promised myself never to go back. I drove to the city's edge and called Linda to let her know I had left. This was the beginning of survival and staying hidden, as I knew he would be looking for me.

John was still required to wear an ankle monitor and still had a curfew. That's why I took his cell phone with me. He couldn't call a gang member to look for me or the car; if he left the property, police would arrest him. I drove to the edge of the city, pulled into a gas station parking lot, and cried. I was truly a mess. Happy, sad, scared all at the same time. I took John's cell phone and looked at his text messages. It was all there. John was very much still doing gang work and, in fact, had been texting the girl I had seen walking that day. I called the number and asked her if she was sleeping with my husband.

The woman was puzzled by my question and asked if my name was Kay. I said yes, and she replied, "John told me you died." That's when the bomb went off in my head. I believed the machete incidents and threats to kill me were not just words and fake actions, or as John said, "playing around." I came to the deep realization that my husband was, in fact, plotting to kill me.

The sickening feeling in the pit of my stomach, coupled with the fight-or-flight mentality, fueled my will to put myself into survival mode. There was no time to process the violence I had been through, only enough room in my head to make an emergency plan to stay alive. I was in a different country, while the worldwide pandemic was at its worst with a stay-at-home order in place, with nothing but the clothes on my back, my passport, and driving John's car. I had not made any friends down here other than one person who had helped me with some odd jobs in his shop to make some money, and his name was Jim Malone. I reluctantly made the call to him, and he told me to get out of the county I was in and to get a hotel room down closer to his county, then I was to call him in the morning.

Morning arrived, and I met Jim at his shop. He knew I was in danger, so he put the car into his shop and allowed me to stay in his office until I could make a better plan. His shop had cameras and an alarm system, so I felt safer knowing that the car was hidden. Jim lived not far from the shop, so it was a good plan. The office had a comfortable couch, fridge, and microwave, and the shop had a shower. I remained hidden for a few days then my cell rang. John's probation officer called and told me John was told he had to leave our home and move to his grandmother's.

I was left with the impression John was gone, and I could go back to the house to collect my clothes and medication. Jim did not think it was a good idea that I drove John's car back there, so he gave me the keys to his minivan. I started back to my house in the van, which was about an hour's drive. As I slowly pulled up to the house there was a woman holding my front door open, but John was nowhere to be seen. I thought someone was breaking into my house. I pulled into the driveway, opened the van door, and screamed, "Hey, who are you? "Get away from my house". As I screamed, the woman took off and started running. I started running after her, but she got away.

As I stopped and turned around, there he was. John came out of nowhere. John started strangling me as I stood in the middle of our front lawn. I fought back, tried to spit in his face, took my nails, and clawed his face, and somehow, I got free. My purse dropped in the altercation, but I forced my way into the neighbor's side door, screaming, "He's going to kill me. Call the police". My neighbors were panicking. They called 911. As I peered through the neighbor's side door window, I could not see John anywhere. I was hyperventilating, and what was going through my mind was to get away. Johns trying to get into the neighbor's other door, I got to get away. If John gets in here, he will kill me.

I took my chance. Police were taking too long. When I parked the van and got out, I left the driver's door open, and the passenger door was only a few feet from the neighbor's. We shared driveways. I opened that neighbor's side door, bolted through the passenger minivan door, climbed into the driver's seat, and started the van. As soon as I grabbed the handle to close the driver door, John was now hanging onto the driver door to get inside the van. I was screaming, get away, get away and he was screaming I'm going to kill you. I slammed the van in reverse and put the gas pedal to the floor. John would not let go of the door. As the van backed down the driveway at a great speed, John and the door slammed into an electricity pole, and the entire minivan door ripped off. John and the door were now lying on the edge of the driveway. I slammed the gear into drive and screeched down the road to the gas station at the end of our road.

Patrons at the gas station also called 911. Police finally came along with an ambulance. My neck was beet red with finger marks. I was hysterical. I was put into the ambulance and assessed.

Police came to talk to me, and one officer said, "John said you are drunk; that's why you hit that pole." I told the police that was a bald-faced lie. John strangled me on the front lawn, and I tried to escape as he hung onto the van door, screaming I'm going to kill you. Next thing I know, I'm being told I would have to take out a criminal summons on my own. It turned out that the woman at my door was John's sidepiece. This woman lied to the police; unfortunately, I did not have a witness.

The police in my county did not help me. Instead, I was scolded and threatened that I could be arrested for a D.U.I. I would have blown zero. However, that chance was never given to me. Instead of the police conducting a proper investigation, they believe John and his sidekick. Sent me on my way. I surely did go to the court house after demanding an officer come with me as I was afraid John would follow. The magistrate did issue a criminal summons, which meant John stayed free until court.

This part of my life was just the beginning of being failed by the people who were supposed to protect and help. The message that I want to leave readers is don't ever give up on the truth and certainly know the strength one has inside to survive.

Exposure to traumatic events can lead to stress, fear, and isolation, which may lead to depression and suicidal thoughts or behavior. Survivors of domestic violence may internalize verbal abuse from their partner. They may blame themselves for their situation or feel anger and resentment toward themselves.

So many times, I felt as though it was my fault for not being under-standing enough, or demanding too much, which only delayed my escape and caused me severe physical and mental harm. My choices to "explain away" how I was being treated almost got me murdered. I was very lucky. I escaped death three times while in the relationship and managed to stay alive for more than a year while he ran the streets looking for me.

My advice is LEAVE. Violence, no matter why it happened, is not love. I spent every moment trying to "fix a man" who was a danger to himself and the general public, and I would go as far as to say in my opinion this man will murder again.

John was eventually charged with aggravated assault causing serious bodily injury, felonious restraint kidnapping, two felony strangulations, three assaults on a female, communicating threats to kill me, and three violations of my restraining order.

After I escaped, John went on and racked up more than 15 new criminal charges, not including mine. Three of those charges were dangerous violent crimes.

My full story of perseverance, the will to survive, victim shaming, the fight with the justice system to stay alive, the investigations, and eventually, what happened to John and where I am now in my life will be told in my own book which I'm working on, but for now, this is a glimpse to all that if you are strong enough to stay in it your strong enough to leave it.

Trust and believe in yourself. THERE'S ALWAYS A WAY OUT. I'm one message away from helping make a plan to leave.

KAY BOHEMIER

"She will blaze through you like a gypsy wildfire. Igniting you soul and dancing in its flames. And when she is gone, the smell of her smoke will be the only thing left to soothe you."

Nicole Lyons

TWO

A Single Mom's Un-Hypnotizing Journey

DANCING WITH QUANTUM EFFICIENCY INTO FREEDOM

"Dancing with reality and imagined desirable futures creates a fast track to a fulfilling magical life."
Jill Fischer

It's 2005. I'm holding my one-month-old daughter in one arm and my three-year-old son's hand in the other as we walk out the door of our family home. I'm numb. I don't know how I feel. I just know that we can't stay here. I can hear my husband yelling from inside our home in a drunken slur, "You can't make it without me!" I swallow hard with tears streaming down my cheeks and keep walking, not knowing how I will make it without him, but I knew I had to try.

I had done everything I knew how to support and love my husband. I was so tuned into his pain and hurt, I desperately wanted to help him. It's like his pain had lived inside me. I didn't know it then, but this is what it's like to be empathic without boundaries. The pain I felt was his, not mine. I later realized that it was up to him to heal himself, not me.

Meanwhile, I had turned myself into a gut-wrenching pretzel trying to make our marriage work and focusing on keeping him alive. He's driven drunk so often that it's a miracle that the only known casualty has been our new Chevy Trailblazer, written off as totaled from him driving into a mountain in the Rocky's. Oh, and then there's the black eye he came home with from being beaten up by his drug dealer after blacking out for a week and burning through thousands of dollars on who knows what.

There are endless stories of the crazy-making antics his drugs and alcohol had him do. It's as if all the drugs and alcohol blanketed over the man I fell in love with. Like blackout curtains hiding the light in his heart, he's gone. All he is now is this irrational, angry, paranoid, jealous, possessive, controlling, misogynist man-form that's crazy, unpredictable, and increasingly dangerous.

So I dug deeper into my denial and deluded myself further into being "the one" who could rescue him. After all he rescued me. He saw me through cancer treatment only nine months after we met. I thought he would be okay if I focused more on him and helped him through this disease, (except he wasn't helping himself) In my misguided conditioning to be a martyr and repeating an inherited past of misogyny, I abandoned myself and all my joys.

I sold my kayak and my two motorcycles. I stopped going to the theatre and opera. My creative flow is vacant, and the full-time artist in me is dormant. I don't exercise. I rarely laugh. I now look androgynous as I've given up being attractive, so my husband doesn't get upset at the thought of possible competition. I have few friends. I mostly stay in my house, being a "good" mom and a "good" wife. I'm depressed and lost. My husband's light has disappeared, and mine is fading fast.

I know I'm not alone in this story: "It takes an average of 7 attempts for an abuse survivor to leave their abuser and stay separated for good." (Bureau of Justice Statistics).

Fast forward: four months after finally leaving him, I'm at a drug rehabilitation center in group therapy for loved ones of addicts. We're sharing in a circle, and I have a light bulb moment: "It's not about him! My life is about me. It's not about saving him. I've been tolerating this abuse and shrinking my life to support what I detest: drug and alcohol abuse and patriarchal oppression." OMG! This is not who I am! I'm clear that I need to change, or I'll unwittingly repeat this pattern and go into another abusive, oppressive relationship.

This is when my insatiable "fix me" journey begins. So, I sign up for personal development courses, counseling, life coaching, shamanism, reiki, mindset programs, law of attraction classes, neuroscience studies, meditation retreats, and so much more. Along the way, I stumble into hypnotherapy and energy healing. I'm blown away! It's like I found the keys to the kingdom.

I quickly realize that I'm not broken and don't need fixing. I just had some incorrect programming. I discovered that there was some un-hypnotizing to do. I was carrying layers and layers of oppressive energy from seemingly endless lifetimes of women conceding to abusive men in order to survive. And, as a woman in this lifetime, I have the perfect opportunity to be free, to be me. We, both women and men, are at a time in the expansion of humanity's consciousness to be fully the gift of who we are. Un-hypnotized, fully awake and aware.

I write these words in 2023, 18 years after walking away from my marriage, with two healthy, well-adjusted children and a flourishing career as a hypnotherapist. My son Ben is finishing his business degree at the University of Victoria and is on his way to becoming a Firefighter. My daughter Cori just graduated from high school and has an intense passion for life as she finds her authentic path. I supported and raised them as a full-time single mom with my hypnotherapy and energy healing business.

Their father hid his money from us (I believe millions) with the help of his father (the children's grandfather). The misogynist pattern is still alive and well on my former husband's side of our family. I choose to flourish forward with or without them.

Again, you likely identify with this story or know someone who has been through this. And despite the common idea that women "take men to the cleaners" and live off their income after divorce, this is not true. "Women who worked before, during, or after their marriages see a 20 percent decline in income when their marriages end, according to Stephen Jenkins, a professor at the London School of Economics. His research found that men tend to see their incomes rise more than 30 percent post-divorce. Meanwhile, the poverty rate for separated women is 27 percent, nearly triple the figure for separated men," writes Darlena Cunha for The Atlantic in April 2016.

I'm currently Founder and President of the College of Holistic Healing (www.chh.online) and inventor of Fischer Formula Colloidal Silver (www.fischerformulasilver.com) while completing my post-doctoral studies in Philosophy with a Masters in Energy Psychology and Clinical Hypnotherapy. I share this not to brag, but to inspire you to be on your journey of who you really are.

I believe that we as women are finding our way into a new tomorrow of being free to be the brilliant, multi-shaped, multi-coloured, multi-aged, limitless, brilliant inventors and co-creators of our future. I believe that gender is fluid and an expression of unique talents and perspectives without compromising our true nature.

You might be tempted to view my abusive marriage story as a catalyst to propel me into being a lightworker and an awesome mom. While I'll take the compliment I just gave myself, this is silver lining think-ing, and it limits us to cause-and-effect Newtonian Physics thinking. As this is a whole other large conversation, in a nutshell, silver lining thinking creates neurology for attaching suffering to our successes. That would mean we must always sacrifice to have joy, love, abun-dance, etc. Not true.

I prefer to see life as a dance of fact and fiction with a metaphysical percussion section keeping rhythm in the background. Being grounded in three-dimensional reality of the facts (void of story or interpretation) while dancing with a multidimensional visualization of a preferred future creates quantum efficiency and eliminates the need to silver line any past suffering.

Dancing with reality and imagined desirable futures creates a fast track to a fulfilling magical life. For example, I was able to leave my husband when I fully accepted the reality of his abuse and my depression. My imagined desirable future was a loving, caring, and safe home with my children. When I walked through the front door, I stepped out of the facts of the abuse and into creating my multidimensional future. Even though it has taken years, I believe I live dancing with quantum efficiency.

Accepting reality gives us personal power and freedom to choose. Healthy boundaries naturally arise from this acceptance. Preferences and values become clear. As we choose to nurture our talents and gifts, we become an expression of our dreams.

What are your dreams?

JILL FISHER

"If you have strength of character, you can use that as fuel to not only be a survivor but to transcend simply being a survivor, use an internal alchemy to turn something rotten and horrible into gold."

Zeena Schreck

THREE

The Will To Live

"If you are always trying to be normal, you will never know how amazing you can be."
Maya Angelou

Well, how do I begin? I want to begin by saying my life story was not a normal one. I'm going to try and convey it the best I can. I know I can't possibly fit everything in. So, there will be gaps. It was a tough road, and I'm grateful to be here still. We all go through things in life, things that sometimes we don't have any control over. This is my story. I wish it were a happier story, but it's my story. So here I go.

I can start off where it all went wrong… My childhood. I was born in the province of British Columbia, Canada, in 1991. The second of five children, two of which were half-siblings, between my mother and father. As a toddler, my dad took my brother and me away from my mother. Both parents had addiction problems. Both parents also had trauma in their childhoods. I should also mention that my mother is First Nations.

My Dad retained custody of my brother and I from there on. We grew up in poverty because of my Dad's addiction and struggles with mental health. Some things I remember are having no clean clothes going through church bins and laundromat bins for clothes. A lot of the time, we had bare cupboards and a fridge, sometimes no food at all. We spent a lot of time standing in the food bank lineups for food and waiting at the welfare office.

There were uncertain times when we would stay in transition houses, and we would lose our home because the rent had not been paid — We lost all of our baby pictures this way. I vividly remember being left in numerous scary and unsafe situations. Once, I must have been three years old, someone broke our sliding glass door, and my brother and I were put into foster care. — I remember being locked in a room in the basement and just being really sad and confused, and I missed my dad.

I felt hopeless in my childhood, but I think it's important to say that when I was with my Dad, there was love. My dad was struggling, but there were times he tried. I remember times when we went camping or to the lake. He brought us on road trips across Canada to visit my grandmother. We went to Canada's Wonderland, and I went on the scariest coaster there. He was there to cheer me on at baseball and school concerts. So, even though there were some really hard and uncertain times, at least I knew what it was like to be loved — I fear this is something my sisters got very little of. They were separated from my brother and me at the ages of two and three. I recognized their need for love as a young girl and tried to be there for them in that way. Even as a kid myself. Figured they needed it.

I remember when I was seven, my Dad somehow got guardianship of my two younger sisters. It really wasn't good timing in terms of how my Dad was doing. I remember feeling responsible for taking care of them because I mostly had to take care of myself. We had no good clothes, so we would steal from the local M.C.C thrift store. (I'm pretty sure the ladies there knew what we were doing but could tell we were in need.) After all, I was seven, and my sisters were ages four and five. We were probably filthy and not to mention all alone downtown. My littlest sister was anything but discreet.

I tried my best as a seven-year-old to take care of my siblings when my dad was in his addiction. I would do Kool-Aid stands and face painting stations so we could get money. One time, this put me in a dangerous situation. My dad was in the house in his room, and I was outside across the street with my younger sisters, and I was having a face-painting stand. When an elderly man with long hair came to get his face painted as a clown, for some reason, I felt sick to my stomach, and something in me made me not want even to touch the man, but not to be rude, I began painting his face. When I was done, he tried to get me to go with him to paint his friend's faces at his house. I told him his friends could come here, I wasn't going anywhere... I had to take care of my sisters. Thinking back to it now, I'm glad I've always trusted my gut instinct.

Eventually, though, there came a day when the social workers came to take my two sisters away from my Dad. They left me and my brother, though. I remember jumping onto the back of the social worker's car and crying my eyes out. I was distraught. I didn't want to lose my sisters. It was pretty hard for a seven-year-old to take.

Around the age of nine when the social worker came to my school to take me into foster care again, I was told of my Dad's suicide attempt. Over the next few years, I was bumped around the system quite a bit, putting me into numerous foster homes. We never returned to my Father's care. After that, my life lacked a crucial ingredient — Love. I never felt loved again. I never heard I love you or am proud of you again.

When I was put into care, I went from not eating properly to having big meals and desserts put in front of me and told to eat as much as I wanted. My foster parents began calling me fat and told me I was overweight. "Face it, Katherine, you're overweight." I was told. I can't tell you how much their comments stuck with me. I really was just a strong and healthy little girl, also starting to bloom faster than the other girls my age. I wish someone had told me there was nothing wrong with me, but I started struggling with body dysmorphia from there on. I would always be wearing baggy hoodies that covered everything but my legs and this accompanied eating disorders. and I was never confident in my skin, always viewing myself as fat, no matter how skinny I got. These problems still affect me to this day.

I also remember wanting to be in dance lessons like my friends and the foster parent's daughters, but I never got the luxury. I often wonder how my life would have been with these opportunities. It's pretty safe to say as a kid I dreaded the future. Often wondering, what was the point in any of this?

Throughout my life in care, I was moved in and out of my younger sisters' foster home. In which we were treated very differently than the foster parent's own children. To me, it felt like we were being punished for being alive. That's about how I can put it. We were not getting the same treatment as these "righteous children", you know, the children who had a right to be there and were actually loved. We were kicked out of the house all day, fed lunch like animals, outside, the last ones to be considered. We weren't even allowed in this house on a rainy day — I asked once. Just once because I got screamed at and told how worthless we were… I remember asking why her children got to be inside, and I was screamed at and told that they weren't little brats like us. We learned never to question anything. On weekends, we were also shipped off to the place we liked to call "The kid farm". In which the conditions were even more deplorable and degrading. We spent most of our summers there.

Despite the cruelty I received, I remember taking on as many chores as I could to try and be loved or appreciated by my foster mother, but it never happened. This hurt so much. Her kids never did anything, never had to lift a finger, and they got whatever they wanted, i.e. (lessons, computers, nice clothes, gym memberships, tanning, and cars on their 16th birthdays.) I remember, as a nine-year-old, writing in my journal that I'd give anything to be them for a day. Just to know what it was like to be loved like that.

Over the years, I kept being moved in and out of this foster home. The foster mom would act loving and kind, so I would think as a kid that maybe this time it would be different, and I'd agree to move back. After all, love was the only thing I wanted or needed. Of course, this was all just fake, and when I was back, the degradation started again. I'm pretty sure she was just after the money. Not to mention, I did a lot of work around there and gladly took care of the other foster children, so why wouldn't she want me back? This led to me not being able to trust anything good that came my way, anytime throughout my life.

I finally had enough and ran away. I'd rather live on the streets than be treated like that any longer. I didn't belong there. I did try as a 14-year-old to get my younger sisters out of this home but it was to no avail. I was afraid for my sister's well-being. I was thinking about their futures. It was a degraded lifestyle. We had nothing to look forward to. I heard that the social workers went there, and my sisters were left there. This life was all they knew. They knew nothing else. I knew they had to get out of there, but who would listen? It was too late, though, they were there, and I was unable to help.

Years later, turns out I was right about what I said would happen to them if they were left there. I said if they were to be left there, the psychological abuse they had endured living like that in MCFD would be too much, I felt like they'd have no will to fight for anything. I can't explain to you what living like that does to your whole sense of self-worth and it turns out I was right.

This has been one of the hardest pills to swallow.

I excelled in school as a younger girl. I want to thank my teachers for being the one true source of any kind of positive feedback or praise in my life at that point. It meant so much to me that someone or anyone believed in me or saw any potential. It wasn't enough, though, to cover or pull me through the hurt buried deep inside me.

A young girl without a mother and left to her own devices. I knew I would have to move mountains to become anything in this life, and it felt like a mountain I couldn't conquer, even with my intelligence. When you are a child, of course, you don't have a crystal ball; everything seems absolute. No Mother or Father. No uncles or Aunts. I was on my own. I never knew in the future that I would ever get an opportunity. I didn't know that as you get older, you have the power to change your reality. Nobody told me. This was it to me. I reached a "fuck it" stage far sooner than any child should have, and no matter how I cried for help, I never got any. I needed a counselor.

This led me to the streets at the age of 12. The streets accepted me. As soon as I figured out a way to escape my reality, I was gone. I ran from my sadness by experimenting with drugs and alcohol at a very young age. Deep down, I knew it wasn't for me though, but, feeling trapped. I just stayed there in the cycle of addiction.

I ran away from the foster home my sisters were in because of emotional and psychological abuse. I ran away from the group homes I was in, too. In my mind they weren't homes. Just places to be where I don't belong. I stayed on the streets. One group home mother would drop me off at a Greyhound with a bus ticket to Abbotsford when I was 13. I was on the street pretty much the whole time I "lived" there. My health and hygiene suffered.

Staying on the streets and couch surfing starting at 12 put me in extremely vulnerable positions. There were times when I wasn't even currently housed, homeless. I would be on the streets late at night, my toes were freezing, and I had no proper shoes. I had sandals. I was alone and cold on the streets with just a bag of belongings. It was raining. I couldn't help wondering why my parents didn't stick it out with us. Why I had to live like this? Often wondering what this life was all about. I don't know what was in me to get me through those days.

Back then, I had a best friend named Chelsey Acorn. She and I would spend most of our days and nights together. We would hug in the cold and sing to keep us distracted from the fact that we were freezing. Chelsey had a very similar life to what I had experienced. We were best friends from the moment we met. Born three days apart in the same year, too.

At the age of fourteen, Chelsey ended up a missing person. I was a part of the investigation to try and locate her, but I knew deep down that if even I couldn't find her, something really bad had happened to her. As time passed, I realized I was correct. I couldn't feel her here anymore. My intuition was right again. It wasn't a year later they found her remains.

At the age of fifteen, I was brought in by I.H.I.T.(police) When I found out who she had last been seen with, I remember becoming flushed with emotion. I knew these men. Chelsey and I had met the older man Jesse "Blue" West together on 1st Avenue in Mission when we were very young. Around 12, I believe. He was in a treatment center one of our friend's boyfriends was in, so that is how he came across us both. I remember not wanting to shake his hand. He gave me the creeps. I believe he decided that very day that he wanted Chelsey and me. We were easy targets.

So, at the age of 14, Chelsey is already missing. It was late on a summer night. I was on the streets and standing at a payphone. I wanted to get back to the group home, but it was past curfew and late at night, and they would not let me come back, nor help me get back. This was when that same creepy man, Jesse "Blue" West, approached me while I was at the payphone. He tried sweet-talking me into coming with him to his place. I was NOT having it. I told him in the most unkind way and very loudly to get away from me. He then called me a fucking bitch and yelled some expletives, then jumped in the same truck Chelsey was last seen in and fled the area. Once again, I was going with my gut instincts. Little did I know at the time I had just saved my own life… again.

The way they got Chelsey was Jesse used his son, who was in his early 20's, to lure Chelsey in. She just wanted to be loved and taken care of. She took the bait. I remember hearing about this and meeting the young one (Dustin) at a bus station, and for some reason, I was immediately disgusted by him and remember telling him, in the most unkind way, exactly what I thought of him and to leave my friend alone.

I didn't know why, but I trusted my gut. My intuition. Unfortunately, I couldn't prevent what was to happen to her. It was Dustin who smashed her skull with a boulder. Thinking back to it now... I'm glad I told him exactly who I knew he was when I did... because I never got to attend the trials. I had no way of getting there and was struggling in so many areas of my life. The details of her death might have been too much for me to witness at that time anyway.

Although I may have escaped the same fate as my best friend, I wasn't spared. During my time on the streets between the ages of 12 and 14. I was raped by multiple men who were far too old to associate with a young girl like me — This is why young girls need to be protected. These men would lure me in and give me affection to get me in a vulnerable position, usually with alcohol and some kind of drug, and then do whatever they wanted to me.

Every time this happened, I kept it to myself. I don't know if it's because I felt or knew nobody would care. I put it away and never thought of it again. One of these instances, in particular, is too much for me to tell, with ugly details that I'm going to leave out this time, but it definitely took its toll.

As an adult, I struggle with shame, often wondering why I allowed these things to happen to me. I've come to realize that affection of any kind was still more than I was getting. This has been a healing realization for me. Realizing my own naivety was a hard pill to swallow, because I feel so foolish, BUT — In realizing this, I can begin to forgive myself.

Again, at the age of 15. The same year, they found Chelsey's remains. I was raped by a group of men that were supposed to be my friends. I thought they had respect for me, and they ended up disrespecting me in the worst way possible, I couldn't tell anyone because they were very connected to my group of friends. Not the nicest people, and being alone and having to take transit everywhere, I felt like I had no chance of pressing charges for fear of the repercussions in my social circle… I was, essentially, alone with no protection.

This led to having to see my friends and family associate with these people for years to come, each time like a stab to my heart, furthering the notion that I was worthless even to the people I loved. Some of them unknowingly did so because I was too afraid to tell them who these men were and too ashamed to admit what they had done to me.

After being raped, I went to the hospital but didn't allow the rape kit out of fear. I knew if I were going to press charges, I would be alone because I truly had no one. It felt impossible. They got away with it.

This next part was complete and utter crap that didn't need to happen, but it did and deserves recognition. After the hospital, I wanted to go to the mall because I had been working and saved up my pay cheque to buy myself a new cell phone. I really had my mind set on this. I was trying to move on with my life. This was my plan the day before they raped me, and I felt like it could ease some of my pain, retail therapy, but when I went to the mall it was closed for Easter. I remember it being a gray, cold day. I hopped on the bus, and within 30 minutes of being dropped off at the mall after the hospital, I was back at my group home.

I remember all I wanted to do was go into my room and call the last person who I believed loved me to cry, but when I asked for the phone, one of the group home workers started accusing me of drinking, which was completely bogus. I was JUST at the hospital with the police and my other youth worker. How could I have been drinking? All I was asking for was the phone, so instead of feeding into her shit, I just snatched the phone from her, and I went into my room. Only to be interrupted 10 minutes later by the other group home worker telling me to pack my stuff because I had just lost my home again.

This was the second home in a year I had lost, and I had no idea why... Then, the police officer who was at the hospital with me came to my room to collect me and take me to the after-hours ministry office to be put in an emergency placement. I was so distraught I asked him why, through my tears, and he just shook his head sadly and told me that some days he hates his job.

Turns out, the first group home worker lied and said I threatened to kill her, but when the police took statements, nobody's statement matched hers, so they refused to press charges. I still lost my home, and my employment, which was a 5-minute walk from my group home, because they shipped me off to White Rock and my job was in Langley, and at the time the commute would have been too long via public transit. We're talking two to three hours of travel depending on traffic.

So, not only was I raped and disrespected by people who were supposed to be my friends, I lost my home, and my employment, was wrongfully accused, and was forced to leave my friends, all in 48 hours. I can't tell you what this does to a young girl who was already tired of fighting and had just previously lost a home and a best friend to murder. It seemed that no matter how many horrible things had already happened, more would come. I couldn't catch a break. Life didn't seem worth living.

I AM, however, grateful for the policemen who stood up for me that day, it's because of them I've never had a criminal record. I often think about the one who was so protective of me when the after-hours social worker, whose name I will kindly omit, came out of the after-hours office, yelling at them to press charges on me and take me to jail. He said "NO ONE, is taking her to jail, NO ONE, is pressing charges, the statements did not match." — and this could have been the first time anybody ever stood up for me in my life.

After all of this, I was moved two more times and then stuck in a group home in the area of Newton. I went into a downward spiral. I didn't plan on coming out of this one. I had seriously given up. Until something changed.

The "something" that changed... I was finally given a chance, almost a year later, and in a new group home I was being moved again, this time into my own placement, with a youth worker only dedicated to working with me. The person who was going to be in charge of the next part of my life was someone I knew loved me. Her name was Marlene, she was an earth angel. I had met her a few years previously. Her work contract was short back then. She was just an emergency worker for me at the time, but the little bit of love she showed me was enough to keep me going, and I would call her from time to time even when she wasn't my worker. She was like a life raft, something good to hold on to.

I FELT RELIEVED when I found out she would be my worker until I aged out. I felt like maybe I was being given a chance; all my dreams and hopes of finding someone to love me like I deserved it had come true. Why didn't it fix me though? Maybe it felt too good to be true?

I was still lost and hurt, and at the age of 16, I tried to kill myself. Even though I finally had the love I needed, I couldn't get over the life I had to endure. This is where God comes in.

It was January 1st, 2008. I was out with my "best friend," who was the wrong kind of person, she knew I was raped, but she shamed me when we wouldn't get along, and she would say things to hurt me, things you can't take back. Things about me being raped. It was really detrimental to me because I was already struggling with the fact that I couldn't bring myself to press charges. I couldn't stand up for myself. Her saying these things to me solidified in my mind that I didn't matter to anyone, not even my best friend. I guess I didn't acknowledge how bad it hurt, but that night, I tried to kill myself after a falling out at a New Year's gathering.

Marlene had come to get me from Vancouver, and the whole ride home I wanted to jump out of the moving car. When we got to the residence, I grabbed two Costco-sized bottles of Tylenol, downed them both, and crawled into bed. I had the idea to talk to God, I boldly asked him if he was real and if I wasn't supposed to die and had a purpose to be here, to do something then, or I'd fall asleep, and it would be over... I'm not kidding you, at 3 o'clock AM my phone started ringing.

The phone call that saved my life. It was a previous youth worker I had called earlier that day to wish a Happy New Year, returning my call at 3 AM while she was celebrating her engagement in Whistler. Go figure. She didn't expect me to answer, but she immediately knew why she had called me. She told me to put Marlene on the phone, and it was like nothing. I was up. I still felt like I wanted to die, though, almost like it was too much for me to bear knowing I was meant to be here. Part of me still wanted peace and finality.

I was put in restraints at the hospital and was given liquid charcoal, which I ended up getting on my expensive brand-new white shoes I had just bought myself from working. I was extremely lucky the Tylenol had miraculously not reached my liver. Even though it was the rapid-release tablets I had swallowed.

When I woke up in the hospital though, I expected to be alone, like always, but I woke up to find Marlene sleeping at the end of my bed. I felt guilty because she had a family. I was just some stupid foster kid that no one was supposed to care about. She might have had a clue as to how much this would mean to me. Or maybe that didn't even cross her mind. Doesn't matter.

Marlene showed me again and again that there was nothing I could do to scare her away or make her not love me. I was so used to being disposed of at that point in my life. I wish her love were enough to make me all better, but the damage had been done. I could not make sense of it because it was all too much. It was just the unbearable sadness I couldn't get away from. In the end, though,

I chose to live, and God began showing me why I couldn't go just yet.

One winter day, I was traveling in the car with a youth worker, and I was praying. I prayed for my mother who I hadn't seen in 10+ years. While praying, and had the idea, or revelation, whatever you want to call it — to try a phone number I was given for my Mom, which, when I had tried calling it before was out of service. Mid-prayer, I picked up my phone and dialed that number, and, to my surprise. It started ringing. The next day, I went for lunch with my Mom. It was hard to see her the way I found her again, but I had plans. I was going to do everything I could to convince her to be clean and sober. So, I started at lunch.

Not long after, I found out one of my younger sisters was kicked out of the nasty foster home she had to grow up in — the one I ran away from. Marlene allowed me to help my sister and take her under my wing... I was trying to save her from going through what I had to go through. It was at this time, as hard as it was for me. I ended up saying to my Mom that she had the chance to have her kids back in her life but that I didn't want to be in her life if she continued using drugs, which is what kept her from me my whole life, and I had gone this long without her.

Thank God, it wasn't two weeks later she was on her way to recovery. She's been a solid person in my life ever since. Fifteen years clean and sober, I love my mom.

At the age of 18, I was given the opportunity to become my younger sister's youth care worker. I tried my best to help her, but the extent of emotional and psychological abuse had taken its toll on her. We still had so many good times together, and I'm so grateful for them all, but at a time. I had to move on with my life. The living arrangement was not working. She wasn't going to school, or trying to get her license, she wasn't trying to find work. I felt like I was putting so much energy into anyone but Myself. I worked five days a week, and she wanted to chill with me or have me do everything for her on weekends, too, and if she did appreciate any of it, she had a funny way of showing it. Or not showing it. It felt redundant.

I try not to struggle with guilt over leaving my job as her youth worker and moving on to my own apartment with a job as a construction flagger. It broke my heart because she was addicted to crystal meth and living in a run-down shack not even a month after I stopped being her worker. After a short time, she became pregnant, got clean, and had my nephew. I thought this might be the thing that would ground her, but I could tell she was struggling and was still trying to run from some of the same feelings I was trying to run from.

Unfortunately, when my nephew was about two years old, my sister became addicted to heroin. This time, I was worried. Worried more than ever. I began to see less and less of my sister. She became so sickly thin. (Less of her). One time I had to just grab her and hug her cause I realized I might not be able to soon. It seemed like everything I had tried to prevent was happening anyway. All of my anger and frustration with her died at that moment.

In 2014, I gave birth to my own child. I was going to be a single mother, and I knew that he would be my whole world. I had to stop trying to save the world and focus on him. I received devastating news, though, a few months before he was to be born, that Marlene's cancer had taken another turn and this time it was serious. I went to see her in the hospital and this larger-than-life, hero of a woman, admitted to me that she didn't know when she was going to die.

I didn't know how to feel. I can't describe it other than a feeling of emptiness. I avoided the idea of not having her in my life anymore, and when she died a few weeks after he was born. I didn't — at the time, fully allow myself to grieve the loss of someone so pivotal in my life, it's been a process. It seemed cruel though, that she had to be the one that was going, but man was I glad to have her for the time I did. She never got to meet my son, but I imagined her there with me. While I was being strong for my newborn baby after her death, I imagined he could see her. I guess it was my way of grieving the fact that she'd never get to meet him. I know she would have absolutely adored him.

In the years following. I had some health problems and cancer scares, but currently, I have been diagnosed with Fibromyalgia, C-PTSD, and, more recently, PCOS. I've had some scary things show up on tests. Throughout this, though, I have tried my best to keep my head above water, being a single mother with health problems and cancer scares. It is tough because I feel so sick, and almost nothing is enjoyable. But nonetheless, I tried to give my son a normal life, and I've been his mother, there for him and loving him for nine and a half years.

In 2019, my world was again devastated. I was dealt a double blow. I was having drinks with "friends" and ended up getting attacked in my home, by someone I had previously known from my days on the streets as a kid. She, without prompting, attacked me jumping on top of my chest, and started beating on my face repeatedly while I was heard saying, "Stop hitting me, I'm not fighting you." by my neighbors. She didn't relent. She hit me until I could see nothing but my vision shrinking into a circle and going black. I woke up hours later on my floor, bleeding and alone with amnesia. I still don't know why I didn't protect myself, but I was, to say the least, completely inebriated, and unable to at that time.

The next day, I woke up, and one of my eyes was looking at the floor, and the pain was unreal. I couldn't remember what happened, due to the amnesia. I decided I needed to go to the hospital. When I arrived there, I was extremely nauseous and started throwing up blood clots that had leaked into my stomach while I was unconscious and then sleeping. I believe it got me in faster.

After they had taken scans of my head, the doctor told me I would need reconstructive plastic surgery. My attacker had broken the orbital floor in my eye socket. While in the hospital, a nurse prompted me with the question of whether I was unconscious at any point during the attack, and that's when the whole attack flooded back into my memory. This is when I decided to press charges. She didn't have to take it this far; she should have stopped before I was unconscious or not fighting back, and now I needed reconstructive plastic surgery. She left me permanently disfigured for life. She deserved to be charged.

Then, a few days later, I'm in for emergency surgery. My mom came to stay with me to help me with my medications as I was obviously not doing well.

I think it was the day after my surgery when we got the phone call. My little sister was dead. She had passed on. She was gone. All of a sudden, my worst fears had come true. My sister was never coming home. I had ultimately failed. I just wanted the best for her.

Just realizing we will never have her back. She can't get better. It hurt like nothing I'd felt before. We will never laugh together until we pee our pants again; she won't be here to see the kids grow up together. Sometimes, things have a way of happening. One way or another. I blamed my foster mom, and respectfully, she was asked not to attend the funeral.

My mom ended up leaving that day, and I remember feeling super alone. Grieving my sister, and healing from surgery. I was also stressed out because it was a week or two before my son's first day of kindergarten. My face was still messed up, and at the time, I could barely stand because my tremors were so bad in my body. It was a living hell.

I don't think I had enough fight left in me at that point, and I didn't want my life to be true. I went on another downward spiral. It was just the way I dealt with things. I did my job at being a mom the very best I could, I always provided for my son like I was never provided for. I do my best to make sure he knows I love him more than anything. He always had clean clothes and the hottest new toys, healthy meals — the kid loves his vegetables. A mom who loves him and tucked him into bed at night reads him stories and prays together.

But on my weekends alone when he was at his dad's. I turned to drinking and partying to escape my reality again. This time, I was afraid for myself because that fight in me seemed to be gone, and the alcohol and drugs made me so physically ill, yet I kept doing it like a slower form of suicide. Keeping in mind, I had had ZERO access to any kind of therapy for anything up to this point.

Enter my relationship, in which I spiraled down probably the furthest I'll ever go. Up until this point, my son had never seen me drink. This was the bottom. I felt like I had no will to fight or live. The relationship was toxic. I couldn't see a way out. I would try and get him to leave my house, but he would never leave.

One time, as I was telling him to leave, he ended up busting two ligaments in my knee, complete tears of my ACL and MCL. He would always say the one thing that scared him about me was that he knew I didn't need him. Now, I needed him. Convenient for him because he got to stay, right? I couldn't walk. I remember, though, that I wanted OUT of that situation. I did try, though, for the sake of what's good in me, to give him the chance to turn his drinking around as I had already quit. He refused. He would go as far as to drink while at work and come home sloshed. I didn't see a future for us anymore. I wanted to change for the better, and he wanted to stay the same.

A few weeks earlier, we had a fight because he came home drunk, and he kicked a flower vase at my face and dug his fingers into my face, causing me to bleed, and I still have the scar. He then threw me down, and I smashed my head on the corner of the coffee table, which left me with a very large lump protruding from my forehead and swollen with a black eye. He told me not to worry about it and not to go to the hospital; thinking back to it now, I should have gone, considering I do have a titanium implant in there.

I struggled with leaving the only person I had and being alone again. After all, even if it was a toxic situation, I had someone helping me. Although the truth was, things were volatile, and he had a whole slew of problems that even I couldn't help him with. Bigger mental health issues than I was equipped to deal with. He would slash himself with knives when I tried to make him leave, and he stabbed himself in the leg once because my son was misbehaving. I'm talking about extreme behaviors. Extreme even to me.

On the night I had had enough, I wanted him out. He attacked me, biting me, punching me, and trying to choke me. I called the police, they arrested and charged him, and he's been out of my life ever since. Now, I was free to heal, to be sober, to change my life for good. I decided if I was going to live — This is not the life I'm going to be fighting for. That's when I believe I truly started living. I decided to quit running and build the life I wanted to live. I quit drinking for good. I even quit smoking for seven months.

At the time, I found the courage to leave him. I felt alone more than ever, but I accepted the help offered to me — I remember how hard it was and how it took a lot of courage and bravery to admit that I needed help finally — Even help getting help, but I'm glad I did. I knew if I were going to have any chance of being healed and living a life I didn't need to escape from, I would need therapy. It was time. I was assigned an outreach worker.

She helped me find a therapist. She helped me throughout the time I was dealing with victim services and helped me keep my ducks in a row. She offered moral support and helped me understand what trauma does to the brain and how trauma response works. She kick-started my healing journey, and I will never regret reaching out for help. I'm so thankful that this time, it was there for me.

She even helped me get my First Nations Status so I can access more therapy for my trauma. I was also enrolled in numerous parenting classes and completed everyone. I was connected with the right agencies for my son's mental health concerns. We got him counseling. (Not excluding the help of others.) She attended I.E.P school meetings to help me remember what was said and to advocate on my behalf. She understood how completely destroyed I was. My nerves are a complete mess due to the amount of grief I've endured in my lifetime, but she never let me give up, and even though she was just a tempo-rary person in my life... She was like another earth angel; once again, I'm just glad I had the opportunity to cross paths with her. Thank you. If you ever read this, I'm sure you know who you are.

I guess they say you are never fully healed until you can tell your story without crying. I'm not there yet, but I will be.

My life story left me with some scars that will never truly heal. Physi-cally and emotionally. Because of my life, I have struggled with depression and anxiety since as far back as I can remember. Constantly living in a state of fight-or-flight. In my life, I have become versions of myself that I still have to heal from. I never got to put down any roots, never had consistency, never knew what to expect. Until I just started expecting the worst.

But, in my life, I also found a strength that cannot be broken by anything, or anyone thus far. In my life, I have come back stronger more times than I can count on both hands. In my life, I have found faith unwavering. I have proof that good things do come to the weary and hopeless and that true beauty is selflessness, and perseverance pays off. If you're struggling, try your best to find the good, and believe in it anywhere and any way you can find it. I think this is one of the main things I've done in order to keep my head up in this crazy life of mine.

My life has taught me that even if — You can't see the full scope of things, everything around you seem dark and uncertain... There is always potential for more. For a brighter day. You must never stop believing in it or your potential to cultivate it, to get out there and find it. Whatever you do, make a promise to yourself to never give up.

As I'm writing this, I am 18 months sober. I am taking better care of myself than I ever have in my life, loving myself, and respecting myself. Currently healing from multi-ligament replacement surgery. I'm super grateful for the surgery and whoever donated my new ligaments.

My son is entering grade four... I am attending therapy regularly, doing EMDR. I'm super grateful to be on this healing journey, and I'm hopeful for the future. My parents are doing well, and both are clean and sober. I believe that once I'm done with my therapy for C-PTSD, I've given myself the necessary time to heal. I still have something to offer this world. Meaning maybe I can manage my chronic illness better once I've taken care of my mental health. Even if managing my mental health is a long, seemingly scary road because it took 32 years to get here, and what I've included in my story is, no doubt, only half of what I've experienced in life... I'm still willing to go that far.

Although I might be a little late getting to this point and I almost didn't make it... I'm still here, and I'm still fighting. The important thing is the fight in me is back. I plan on healing and creating a successful life for my son and me. I hope that one day, I can be a source of strength for those with similar backgrounds to mine.

You really can keep going even if you can't see a way out of the darkness. I hope this story reaches those who need to see it.

In my life, it is important to me to note that I have been blessed to cross paths with many beautiful Women Like Me. Beautiful women who have inspired me to follow the goodness in my heart and to believe in myself first. Women like this — and I'm not excluding the men like this either — But women like this mean so much to the world. They are the true heroes in my world. That is the reason I kept fighting. They have inspired me to work on becoming who I was truly meant to be. Even if I'm not there yet. Thanks to them, people like me choose to get up and fight another day.

So, thank you, beautiful Women Like ME. Never stop loving with all your hearts because Women Like ME would not be here today without YOU!

KATHERINE WELLS

"The way to right wrongs is to turn the light of truth upon them."

Ida B. Wells

FOUR

The Desire To Do Better

WHY CAN'T IT HAPPEN?

"I came from an "ain't gonna happen" mentality to a why can't it happen? Every time I start a new business or book a trip, I pinch myself and think it's real. I worked for that!"
Lisa Huppée

Throughout my life, I have felt a real connection to nature, especially during challenging times. I feel my journey to becoming my fullest self is like a flower going from the bud stage to the blooming stage. There are still areas I am budding and growing in and others where I feel I am blooming and feel proud of the journey that has gotten me to where I am.

For the majority of my life, I have felt stuck and unsure. I have had to remind myself that becoming my fullest self takes time, energy, hardships, and help along the way. Some people have supportive friends and families. I did not. I know I am not alone. When the people in your life who are supposed to love and support you don't have your back in life, you learn to control whatever you can in your life. Trusting others is a challenge.

As a young woman, I had goals and ambitions to have a good, happy life. Looking back at my 56 years on earth, I have had many struggles and challenges in life, but despite all that, I have overcome a lot.

I have found my life path, helping people and having my own successful business. I am at a stage in my life, as a businesswoman and a person, finally, where I feel I am coming into my own and blossoming.

As a younger person, I was shy and worried about what everyone thought of me and was saying about me. I grew up with a hypercritical mother who was never happy with what I did in life or with me as a person. I had a warped sense of self, my looks, my abilities, and my worth. It has taken me decades to peel back the layers of negativity I was encased in. When you only hear a limited version of a story, you don't have a full picture of the book.

I look back on having figure skated for 10+ years, reaching the gold test level, and remember that my parents couldn't make an effort to ever watch a practice, test, or competition. Figure skating was something my mother wanted to have done as a girl, and I was lucky to have parents who would pay for me to do that sport. It kept me extremely busy year-round.

I would have been involved in my kids' activities as a parent. Other parents were there every practice, etc.... mine were always too busy, and I never did quite good enough to gain their love and respect or even to have them say they were proud of me. I am grateful for what figure skating taught me as a person, but it was not my dream. It was my mother's dream. My worth was based on my achievements and how I made my mother look. My mother wanted to be a figure skater, but with seven kids in her family, she wasn't able to.

I was a people pleaser who no matter what I did or tried, ever felt like I belonged as a family member or was accepted for who I was. I always felt like the odd one out, the inconvenience. My parents had a much different relationship with my younger sister. She wasn't pressured to take sports or classes. She was not pressured to succeed, but she was a smart, talented child. As a parent, I looked back on the openly displayed favoritism and promised never to do that to my own children. The sting of being the "lessor" child lingers.

Having a controlling mother was a challenge but it wasn't until I was a young adult that I understood my father. One of my only memories of a real conversation with my dad when I was a young adult, around 19 years old, was him relaying that he never felt he could get close to me. He stated he wanted a son and that it was very disappointing to have had a daughter. The fact that I did everything a son would do, like painting, building fences with him, mowing acres of grass weekly, etc... apparently didn't matter. I was a disappointment to him.

I also found out that he felt I was not his child. My parents both had dark brown hair and brown eyes. I was a strawberry-blonde child with greenish hazel eyes. So, years of me feeling like a rival or inconvenience were now explained. I now know that when people make you feel small, less than, or unworthy, that is their issue. Know that you are worthy of joy, happiness, and peace... the good in life.

Feeling worthy of care by others has been an ongoing struggle throughout my life. As a child growing up, there were never compliments or accolades. I don't remember my parents saying they were proud of me for anything. Accepting compliments is painful. I'm getting better at listening to compliments, but it's still a challenge to really take them in and feel I deserve the sentiment.

I recently had lunch with girlfriends I have known for 23-plus years, and at lunch, my friend and former boss, Deb, who had recently lost her husband and had a heart attack after moving back to the lower mainland, looked over at me with love and said," Girlie, you are impressive. You should be proud of what you have accomplished. I'm proud of you." My other friend Carol chimed in as well. I smiled, unable to really let that sink in. That day, Deb reiterated the same thing twice during our outing. It was like she knew it wasn't sinking in. She was so genuine and proud. I smiled and said, "Thanks, Deb."

It wasn't until I reflected on what she said two days later and I got teary. Why did I have that wall up? I realized I didn't know how to deal with someone telling me they were impressed with me or proud of me. I subconsciously block positive comments. This was a powerful realization for me that I was so conditioned to persevere and do better, without any positive reinforcement, that I go numb inside (disbelief, I guess) when anyone says anything nice to me.

Deb and Carol are women around my mom's age, who are genuine, caring, and women of strong values. Why couldn't I have had a supportive person like Deb or Carol as a mom growing up? How would I have turned out with some emotional support in my life? I have been worthy of motherly/parental love all along. Some people are lucky to have it, and others are not. You can't make anyone love or care about you. You can only treat others how you want to be treated and be an example of good. Thanks, Deb and Carol, for the lesson. I am good enough. I am me!

Fast forward to me at forty years old. My married life of twenty years had come to an end. Sometimes in life, no matter how much you love a person or want them to change for the better, the result is unchangeable. Having had a heart attack in his later thirties, my now ex-husband wanted to be married for all the good parts but be single and have a secret life of partying and doing drugs. It was a struggle for years, with lies and short "good" periods, where he would take up where he left off, hiding his "other" life and disappointing his family repeatedly. It was a heartbreaking time in my life.

My ex-husband embodied a life of self-indulgence and lack of care for how his actions affected his children and the life we worked so hard for. I was done and wanted out, no matter the financial consequences. For my sanity, it needed to happen.

Change, big change was happening. It was embarrassing and scary. People judged me, for I guess, thinking I lived his lifestyle, which I did not. I lost long-time friends. My church was unsupportive. I thought that's why people are part of a church community to help guide them to make safe decisions. I was mistaken. That was disappointing on many levels, as I felt utterly alone.

I had no family to talk to (my parents had been estranged from me for over 15 years at this point). This was an all time low in my life. At the time, I felt trapped in a job, working for a boss who hated me, blocking me from transferring to a different work location. I felt trapped in every part of my life, literally. I was stressed so much that I walked into a coworker's office and said I was having trouble breathing. I could barely get words out. I felt pressure on my chest. She looked at me and said you must get to the hospital. It sounds like you're having a heart attack. I went to the hospital. They did heart tests, blood tests, you name it... It was stress! Your body knows when things are bad for you. It was a wake-up call.

Change causes suffering. We suffer when our life doesn't work out how you expected, when a relationship ends, or when you have to move and start over. I experienced all the changes I could take in a very short amount of time. I had my ex calling me, telling me how he would kill himself every day for months. I had walking pneumonia while I worked three jobs. The stress of my life caught up to me. It was negatively affecting my health.

I made a pact with a girlfriend going through her own divorce hell, to be there for her and despite intolerable days, be able to celebrate small victories and laugh at life and the ridiculousness that can happen when in survival mode. I looked for the good in life. I did not want to become a bitter old lady like my mother telling people life isn't about having fun!

One thing I learned about life is that, like nature, change is inevitable. Trees deal with the season's changing. Just like nature, we have the ebb and flow of seasons of life with their changes and challenges. I have learned to embrace life with grace and gratitude for the good things, no matter how small. I see change as an opportunity. When one door closes, another five open. (This is a motto that hangs behind my desk in my office.) You must move the things that are not working in your life out to make room for better things to come in and change your life for the better.

My divorce finally happened, and I literally felt like I was finally free and had to literally start my life over. It felt like a mid-life crisis. My ex told me he wasn't attracted to forty-year-olds. Well, that hit me. There I was forty and having to be out there in the dating world as someone who was apparently unattractive. I felt I knew I wanted a better life and what I was and was not willing to have in my life moving forward.

I read the Boundaries book, and that was the start of Lisa coming back. I felt along the way, I lost focus of my inner self, my goals, and my inner happiness to try to keep my family stable. I felt the realization that I failed at my marriage. One person trying to make a marriage work will never be successful. I released the guilt I felt. The sense of relief and new inner peace grew when I could distance myself from the dysfunction and neediness/ manipulation of my ex-husband.

I felt like a baby bird taking its first flight, following its natural instincts, as it leaps from a tree or ledge to experience its first taste of freedom. My instinct told me you can do it, and it's time. I learned from this experience that when your gut tells you... You are ready, don't hold back from taking that leap in your life. Your intuition guides you. Trust and listen to yourself.

We all outgrow things in our lives: hobbies, friendships, spaces, and other things. As we live, we evolve, learn, and try new things. Did I know it was the right path at the start? No. I knew it would be hard, but I wasn't a quitter. Like the hermit crab that outgrows its shell, sometimes in life, you must wriggle free of the constraints that hold you back. Give yourself permission to set yourself free when you are ready to let go.

Having felt the peace and resilience I had moving out of a bad place in my life into a more stable situation, albeit working 2-3 jobs to pay bills and support my kids. I could be bitter about having had to work so hard, but it made me stronger, and more determined to be a good person, a strong woman. Knowing I was completely on my own with no one having my back was one of the most difficult struggles personally. I hated ever having to ask anyone for help, especially financially.

At a low point when my school position was off for the summer while looking for work and having paid all the bills I could afford at the time, I had to use the food bank. I couldn't get any financial help as I had a job but was laid off for the summer. Life felt hopeless and so unkind for someone who wanted to work. It was a defining moment.

In that low, I told myself I will work however hard I have to, to avoid that humiliation of begging for dried-out bread and a few cans of lentils and canned vegetables. Food I wouldn't feed my dogs! It took resilience to be able to eventually shed the negative feelings I had about myself at that time and situation.

Moments like this shaped me but didn't define me as a person. I never lost myself and my vision of having a happier, more secure life. Difficult emotions do not need to be part of our stories Like clouds floating in the sky, challenges are passing experiences. I learned to look at challenges like this without judgment, learn from them, then let them go. I am the most judgmental person to myself. We can be too hard on ourselves. Valuing your worth is important!

I feel if I had given up, gone on welfare, stopped pushing myself to grow and become a stronger person, I would be stagnant. I would never have met Lisa, the owner of six growing businesses, remarried, with puppies, living in a house in the mountains, driving a convertible, and living the life I always wanted. I came from an "ain't gonna happen" mentality to a why can't it happen?

Every time I start a new business or book a trip, I pinch myself and think it's real. I worked for that! Nature reminds us that every day holds the possibility of a new personal victory. Allow these moments of accomplishment to remind you of your strength and resilience. Every day, it's important to note some small personal victories. It could be something you learned, tried, or a challenge you overcame. I am grateful for my journey and desire to do better, help others, and make a difference as a person, employer, and business owner.

Like a flower, my business is starting to bloom, showing the beauty and commitment to helping others through what I do. I employ 250+ people at this moment and want it to be where staff love to work and feel appreciated and valued. Being able to offer free quality training and benefits and an opportunity to grow with the company is something I am proud to offer as an employer. I am always surprised when people turn away from real opportunities that could improve their lives. But that is the beauty in life: having choices to follow your path.

One of my biggest challenges is dealing with people who feel life owes them something. Life is what you put in! No one owes you anything. My best advice to someone wanting to be successful in business is it's not a clock-punching job. No one pays you overtime. No one says wow, you stayed till 9 p.m. to ensure everything got handled. Work for someone else if you want a Monday to Friday 9-5 job with guaranteed vacations and benefits.

I feel like having had to "figure stuff" out continually throughout my life, coupled with not needing outside kudos from others to do my job well and be equipped to be a business owner. I know a lot of people expected me to fail. That is what drives me to wake up every day and push through the "tough" parts of owning a business and dealing with difficult people and situations. I am a female entrepreneur. I have had a complicated life.

I think it would surprise many people to know the challenges and the lows I have faced in my life. I am a private person and don't typically share the weaknesses and struggles that I have lived. I do this as a way for fellow women, no matter what age or current situation, to know whether you are twenty, forty, or sixty, you can change your path/life with determination, hard work, and resilience.

Nature is always changing and adapting over time. As a water sign, Cancer, I feel connected to water and its silent power. It has the ability to transform landscapes, carving out canyons, while having the gentle grace to be calming when watching the rhythm of the waves lapping in on a beach. Water teaches us anything is possible with time and tenacity.

Persistence is a trait that both water and I have. Like water, I commit to moving through obstacles to attain what I set my mind on. I love the fluidity of water. If you can't go head-on and get the desired results, swirl around the problem, finding a different angle to tackle it. Life has taught me to persist like water. The key to my success is the ability to adapt and persist.

LISA HUPPEE

"The success of every woman
should be the inspiration to another.
We should raise each other up."

Serena Williams

FIVE

Will This Pain Ever Go Away?

I THOUGHT MY PAST DESTROYED ME, IT ONLY GAVE ME STRENGTH

"You never know how strong you are,
until being strong is the only choice you have."
Bob Marley

We fell deep in love, the vindictive kind. We came from two different worlds and managed to build an unexplainable strained relationship. Joseph and I were addicted to one another and loved to party; this unique, intense intimacy produced such an ineffable feeling.

I thank God for his protection over my life. He stayed by my side as ugly as I was while under the influence and distracted from life's priorities. Where I come from, I was taught to pray and believe in God's love and healing. And....I'm pretty sure my grief and messy life had God get up and say, "Okay, that's enough," and now has me courageously telling my story.

When I met Joseph, he was a showstopper and eye candy, and his sex drive was immaculate. He stood 6 feet tall, with muscles that had stories told by everyone who knew him, tattoos that complimented his chest and bold arms, his face had high cheekbones, a jawline that put him on the map, and eyes that had this noticeable outline complimenting his beauty. He wore athletic clothing, and his physique stood strong.

He didn't give a shit what people thought; he had friends from all walks of life close to him; few were considered like brothers, and the respect they gave each other showed; he was given recognition anywhere he went in this city, there was always a story of his colorful past.

I was deeply invested in this fantasy of having a fairytale love story; I would meditate and get a satisfying buzz picturing him and I becoming successful, living in a home we called our own, and being "just us." Those daydreams fed me lies, a paralyzed soul holding onto empty promises.

My story looked like a humorous parody of Hansel and Gretel. We were never on the same page; the breadcrumbs were reminders of why we were in this relationship. When we got lost in the sauce, those reminders were gone, and all we had was just us in that moment.

My spirit was smart and used pebbles to remind me where home really was. On May 7, 2020, after an altercation, body shame, and word vomit, he told me to leave. Normally, I would move on as if nothing happened, but not this time. This time, as I sat at the edge of our bed with this excruciating pain in the pit of my stomach, this pain was coming from my soul, and whatever little faith I had left in me gave me the courage to call home.

My new journey started in the summer of 2020. I moved back to my family home, completed a new postsecondary certificate, and was surrounded by the love and laughter of family and friends. I woke up each day in God's beautiful creation of nature, far away from the concrete jungle, and my faith in "hope" was in full effect; this girl was on fire!

Blessings and life were starting for me; I was building my own foundation, finally thinking of my happiness and daydreaming of my success. I got my first apartment and was feeling confident in my new chapter.... or what I thought was my new chapter.

January 2021, I was preparing for my final weeks of school. I was living on my own, the COVID-19 pandemic interrupted family visits, and loneliness was my best friend.

I was waiting for a city bus, and just my luck, my bus was late; the winter air was crisp, and the snow seemed to silence the noise around me. I watched this guy run across the street, and as he got closer, this intoxicating thrill filled my body. He walked towards me flirtatiously; he knew what he had lost and was on a mission to get me, and that he did.

This was now the beginning of our final chapter together.

Joseph was a risk taker, and I was "the one that got away." I don't know where he was originally going that day, but seeing me in person made him drop everything to pursue me. He got on my bus, pretending he was going in my direction. As my stop approached, I said, "Well, this is me, bye." He jumped up and acted like he missed his stop or was near his made-up destination.

When I sat next to him on the bus, after months of being apart, everything inside me was vibrating, and without hesitation, I let him come home with me.

Our first encounter ended up being a weekend of passion that we always had for one another. This agreed one-time visit turned into a secret life I kept from my family and friends for a whole year. I know they knew, but nobody ever talked about it. And as for me, I was back to being in denial, accommodating him and his needs so "we" could be happy.

The honeymoon stage was over, and history repeated itself. He would spit word vomit at me in anger because he couldn't control me like before. I tried my best to stand my ground, not allowing him to take advantage of me; until he found his manipulating blackmail ways to win, I was once again no longer the pack leader in my life.

Joseph's addiction intensified, and he was hiding his method of drug administration. My intuition and love for him was strong. It led me to discover the truth; with little judgment, I just wanted to ensure he was safe. The darkness in my home was heavy, and once I knew why this was. I searched my home; my first sweep, I was in utter shock and disbelief that this was happening and how many I found.

It was soul-shattering to witness his body, mind, and soul deteriorate. Our forced relationship was bitter and getting worse, but both of us still refused to let go. I cried many times, begging God to give me the strength to leave him alone, but no. I feel like I was stuck there because he needed true love.

Joseph walked out of my apartment at 1:30 a.m. on February 9, 2022; he was on day four of an Opioid binge, hallucinating with a muddled mind. The evening prior, he would come in and out of his "nod" and each time say, "This is going to be the last time you'll see me, Hannah!" or (gasp) "Something told me I'm gonna go before Valentine's Day." He tried to manipulate me with his words by saying he had nothing to live for because I wouldn't let him move into my new apartment or tell my parents we were back together.

He stood in my kitchen with tears in his eyes; when I tried to kiss and hold him, he pushed me away with force, saying, "I don't deserve this; you don't love me anymore," and got dressed to leave.

His last words to me as he stood at my doorway were, "Well, babe, at least you got to see me before Valentine's Day." With his arms out like a bully, we stared into each other's eyes, and at this moment, there was a loud silence that draped over him and I. This moment gave me a deep, indescribable emotion.

Joseph died hours after leaving my apartment that early morning. His passing made me feel like I was dying. I was numb everywhere but also in excruciating physical and emotional pain. My life went dark, and I relied on party substances to mask my pain. All I could think of over and over was how he was all alone.

The next three days after he passed, I chose to stay alone in my apartment because I felt him all around me and all over me. As I lay lifeless in my bed, I sensed his spirit get up, and I yelled, "BABE!! NO!! WHERE ARE YOU GOING? STAY WITH ME! KISS ME!" At that moment, I would feel this vibration on my face and along the left side of my body.

My deep connection to him wouldn't let him go anywhere; his spirit then sat on the floor next to me, I was on his side of the bed with my arm extended out. With another painful scream, I yelled, "BABE! KISS ME!! HOLD MY HAND!" Again, I felt a vibration on my face and hand I had extended out.

My overplayed memory of my first night without him, feeling his kisses and touch. I could smell him. I popped my head up, and there he was, sitting next to me. I was in shock but not afraid. I was face to face with my dead boyfriend. I couldn't see his lips moving; he had a sympathetic look on me, and then I heard him say in a heartfelt tone, "Hannah, I'm here; rest. I'll stay until you fall asleep. I'll be here when you get up."

I was angry and in a rage. I yelled at him for pushing me away, letting me stumble to the floor, for not kissing me one last time, and saying I didn't love him! Before falling into a deep sleep, I wept and said, "YOU WERE ALL ALONE!"

When I woke up the next afternoon, I walked into my living room, wearing his house coat that I fell asleep in. I stopped, I don't remember being afraid, but there he was sitting on my couch, and said, "Hi Babe, told you I'd be here when you got up." I fell to my knees and crawled, trying to touch him, but he was gone in a split second.

Saturday, February 12, 2022, I had $18 and got takeout. While ordering my sandwich, out of habit, I asked what soup they had; it was cream of broccoli, his favorite. I got home sensing his spirit. I spoke to him as if he were there: "Hey babe, I got your favorite."

My table was still the same as the night he left: the chair, his empty cigarette package, an empty, twisted tea can, an unopened bottle of water, and the last joint he rolled and smoked. I placed his food where he sat, and I ate my sandwich in silence, then napped on my couch.

I woke in the night, I cried and called for him; he was standing in my kitchen, and I once again heard him say, "Rest, Hannah, you need to rest." His spirit then walked through my fridge and was gone. I wept till I fell asleep.

That morning, I didn't feel him. The food I left on the table fed his spirit, and he left. He still makes it known that he is with me in dreams and signs. My mourning continued to be painfully numbing; there was unnecessary treatment towards me from his family, and to this day, I only have communication with his children and their mother.

God's grace

I became more aware of my struggle and recognized that I needed to get better. I know God and the Holy Spirit nudged me to start my healing journey through journaling and God's word.

Everyone handles grief in their own way. I self-sabotaged my health and mental state, masking my pain. I had a shattered soul, and I felt empty and alone. I was mourning my way. I admit I am stubborn; I always dance to the beat of my own drum.

Bible verses and relevant podcasts were waking me up at night. God saw my broken heart and knew I had it in me to trust in his love and blessings, but I felt so unworthy to accept his help because I wasn't healthy.

God knew I needed soul food and taught me to seek healing through his word. In Proverbs 4:20-22(AMP), God tells us to pay attention to his words, keep them dear to our hearts, and learn from them as they are healing and healthy to us.

My hurt and anger went in all different directions; I was so mad. After all the emotional abuse, infidelity, and humiliation Joseph put me through, I needed to know why I had this deep, unconditional love for him. I was then guided to Leon Fontaine's book, The Spirit Contemporary Life; he references Proverbs 20:27; in paraphrase, he says, "Holy Spirit will lead you to the truth, and you'll feel it deep in your belly."

Joseph never knew God and the love he has for each of us; I never pushed my faith on him, and he respected my beliefs. In 1 Corinthians 13, it tells the love story; it reminds us to stay committed to God's grace through faith, hope, and love. The greatest of these is love. God knew my heart; he knew that I was so lost and sad; he brought me comfort.

The Holy Spirit continued to guide me to God's word and helpful messages.

I will forever be thankful for TD Jakes and his ministry. My wellness journey was and still is guided by his teachings. He reminded me that God created me to be me and not to have a heart full of grief, to stay committed and trust the process.

I showed Joseph love and loyalty in every way I possibly could; I didn't retaliate and expect anything in return. Nothing I did was good enough. I tried to hug and kiss him the night he left, but he pushed me away forcefully with rejection. Joseph tried manipulating me, telling me I didn't love him when I did, then walked out abandoning me, traumatizing me, and that played in my mind over and over. This hurt ran deep.

In one of TD Jake's messages, "Strap: Surviving the Trauma of Rejection and Abandonment Plan," he reminded me that Jesus was rejected.

He came to this world and wasn't recognized. Jesus teaches us that rejection gives us direction.

Grief hits each of us in different ways; smells, songs, movies, and emotions sneak up on us like it was the first day you were told your person left for the spirit world.

December 2022, Joseph's passing still influenced my life and emotions. For healing, I needed a new environment, and fate led me to a new apartment in my building, I blessed my neighbor, who is a young single mother, with my furniture that had memories of our life and bought new ones.

Even though ten months had passed, my heart was hung up on how he was all alone in the end. God knew I replayed different scenarios in my mind and thinking of all the "what ifs." While packing my kitchen, I broke down.

I replayed the night he left me. I was crying with deep emotional turmoil and yelled, "You were right here! I tried to kiss you, and you pushed me away!"

I was now in a fetal position, pain everywhere and tears flowing like a waterfall. Out of exhaustion, I somehow fell into a deep sleep. I hope to think it was the Holy Spirit who gave me a vision that night.

In my dream, I was in the operating room with Joseph, watching doctors perform CPR on him. I stood to the right side; he was facing my way with eyes open, and his right arm was extended out, wearing the blue tracksuit from that night. The doctors were cutting his clothing and defibrillated his chest. Joseph went into cardiac arrest, and in my vision, I watched him take his last breath. Call me a crazy widow, but that moment and our soul tie, I could feel all his pain and sadness released in his body.

During my moving process, I came across one letter he wrote me in 2019 while he was incarcerated; on the back, he wrote, "Out of pain comes purpose, and out of devastation comes direction." I had mixed emotions about my dream and this letter but accepted both as clarity and encouragement to grow through grief.

Now what?

I am now going through a transformation, rebuilding my life's foundation and new identity; I still encounter situations that try to stop me from growing.

I manifest my future to be successful, to accomplish great things, and to use my grief as a ladder to be amazing. I keep this scripture dear to my heart: Joshua 1:9 (NIV), "Be strong and courageous, do not be afraid; do not be discouraged, for the Lord your God will be with you wherever you go."

I like to reference the book of Joshua in my journey to an amazing future. Joshua is scared to be a leader but is encouraged by God that he will do great and will magnify him in the eyes of the people. As Joshua leads the people, they're faced with a flood. As a new leader, he could have given up on the people, but no, God saw his heart and determination, and when crossing the Jordan River, the rushing waters stopped, and they crossed.

Everyone who is trying to overcome life's storms and impediments could let the flood waters take them downstream. I learned that the flood season in life's situations is preparing us for our Harvest- good fortune, success, and love, our promised land.

Many things have happened since Joseph's passing: floods have come in many different areas of my life; longtime friends deceived me. Family members have publicly embarrassed me, bullied me, and spit word vomit on my growth, and in recent months, my best friend Sam left this world.

My wellness journey continues, and it is just like the biblical story of David. David went from being disrespected by the ones he loved, attacked by enemies, and even killed a giant; he was a great warrior, and God gave him the skill to win every time. Through it all, he never thought he would be where he ended up. With David winning each fight, it was God preparing him for his destiny and was crowned a king.

I will fight each fight that comes my way. I will never give up and forever trust in God's preparation process.

It might not be tomorrow, next week, or next month. But when the time comes, I know my promised land and crown of jewels will be my new life filled with love, laughter, and success, and each will come without force.

I would like to wholeheartedly say Miigwich (Thank you) to my parents and the few friends who still to this day show their support in my wellness journey. These girls were in constant contact with me when I lost Joseph. They sat with me, fed me, and wiped my tears. I love you all.

HANNAH THURIER

"I declare to you that woman must not depend upon the protection of man, but must be taught to protect herself, and there I take my stand."

Susan B. Anthony

SIX

My Mother Who Couldn't Love Me

MENDING THE BOND THAT WAS NEVER THERE

"To feel that you aren't important to your mother leaves a hole. Most
often, it is felt as a hole in the heart.
It's the hole where Mother was supposed to be."
Jasmin Lee Cori

I was in therapy at the time I wrote this story about my mother. I have
had much trauma in my life over the years, and this particular story
was instrumental in my recovery process. At the time, I was diving
into the book 'Mothers Who Can't Love' by Susan Forward, recommended by my therapist. It not only fascinated me to learn that I was
slowly slipping out of the victim role but that I was also able to see my
mother's behavior for what it was...depressive, encouraging lifelong
rivalries between the siblings, and her failure to protect me from my
father.

I could finally see that my countless attempts to get her attention
through good grades, cleaning the house, or being submissive would
never have made a difference. It wasn't a me issue; it was a mom issue.
She was often in a depressed state of mind, unavailable, neglectful,
and unaffectionate. Although I have realized that her inability to show

affection was likely due to her upbringing as a child, I just felt like she didn't like me and that I was not loveable. Love was never given or shown. Though my attempts were never recognized, I always thought I had to earn it. I wondered what my friends did to get their moms to sit them on their laps and hug them. I would have given anything to see that look of love on my mom's face when she looked at me. If I had only seen it being mirrored, I'd have felt more comfortable knowing how to give it.

I witnessed things as a child that you can't erase. Things I saw my mother do. I saw her daily on a basis…. not connected with the real world. I knew with great certainty that what I saw was unsettling and indifferent, yet I knew better not to speak to anyone about it. They were family 'secrets.'

I remember my 1st day of kindergarten like it was yesterday. My mom and I walked two blocks to the school. I was nervous and excited at the same time. My older sister and brother had been attending school for two to three years, and I wanted to go, too.

My mom and I entered the little cloakroom, and I saw other children and their moms. I was enthralled by the interactions between the moms and their children. I watched as they hugged their children and showed them how to hang up their book bags. Some moms even carried their children into the building and entered the main room together.

The room looked huge to me, and I was scared to go in. My mom told me to hang up my bag, and 20 seconds later, she was gone. I stood there, afraid to move for a moment, and followed another little girl and her mom into the big room. Several play stations were set up…a sandbox, painting area, blocks, mats on the floor, books on a shelf, and a dress-up area. I wasn't sure what to do. I waited for someone to tell me what to do, like usual.

While I was looking around, the teacher, Mrs. Pettingill, came over and squatted in front of me. She took my little hands in hers and asked me my name. I was stunned. She was touching me....and smiling at me! My first reaction was to pull away. The closeness of her face so close to mine made me feel uncomfortable, yet her smile made me feel important. I couldn't believe she was 'seeing' ME.

The only problem I had with kindergarten was nap time. All the other kids got onto their mats, laid down, and closed their eyes for 30 minutes each day. I sat on my mat, afraid to close my eyes in case someone touched me. I don't think I understood who might be wanting to touch or hurt me, but I always felt safer keeping my eyes open.

I had asked Mrs. Pettingill several times if she would teach me how to read. She told me I would learn to read next year in grade one. My older sister was bringing home books from her grade one class, and sometimes, she would let me read with her and help me sound out the words. I wanted to read just like her. I begged my teacher to show me how, and she eventually relented. So, during nap time, two to three days a week, she would sit with me, and we would read. Books gave me a window into another world I couldn't get enough of. That world was so much more comforting than my own. It allowed me to escape.

During my teen years, my mother babysat other people's children during the day. I would arrange my high school schedule, giving me an extra long lunch break so I could go home and help my mom with the babies. I loved being around them. I liked seeing their excitement and smiling faces in response to seeing me arrive. It was a good feeling to have someone so excited to see me, even if they were only infants.

At the time, my mom was looking after 6-month-old Jason and 14-month-old Peter. I walked in one day to find Peter crying uncontrollably. My mother's actions showed me she didn't like Peter as much as James. She very seldom talked to him or offered him any encouragement when he was doing something good. I was used to that, but it still felt odd that she couldn't muster up a little love for these sweet little boys.

That day, when I got home, Peter was crying because he was over-tired and just wanted his sippy cup. My mother wouldn't give it to him, and when I offered to take over and feed him, she blew up at me. Then my mother picked up the sippy cup of milk, removed the lid, and said, "You want your milk, Peter, here it is," and dumped the whole cup of cold milk over his head. Peter could hardly breathe. He was trying to gulp in air while crying hysterically.

I scooped Peter out of the high chair and spent the next 30 minutes washing him down, changing him, then cuddling him to calm him down. I took the time to rock him to sleep, making me late that day for my next period at school. I didn't care.

I babysat Peter occasionally in the evenings or on the weekends, and it was not uncommon for me to drop in and visit him. The next evening, after school, I stopped at their house to see Peter. His mother told me that Peter showed signs of agitation in the mornings when she dropped him off at my mother's. She said she didn't know what to think of it. She thought maybe he was showing extreme signs of separation anxiety and wasn't sure what to do about it.

Without trying to give anything away, I suggested that the environment at my house was not good to be raising a child in and that perhaps she should start looking for another sitter. She tried to press me for examples of why she shouldn't leave him with my mom, but I told her only that my mother suffered from depression and wasn't always at her best. She found another sitter, and I was able to continue to see Peter.

I also never quite understood why my mother ignored my dad's inappropriate sexual behavior with us. She would not listen to us when we told her what was happening. It was like she didn't care. How could she not see that it was wrong for my father to be peeking into our bedroom window at night while we were changing for bed?

How could she not see that he was pulling our pants down to age 14 to spank us? How could she leave us alone with him when she went to bingo, bowling, or her art painting classes? I remember begging her to take me with her when she went out in the evenings. I told her that I could keep score for the ladies at bowling, help her carry her art supplies, and help her set up at her oil painting classes. Sometimes, I got to go. Maybe the thought of me as useful to her convinced her. I didn't care as long as I got to go.

It was nice, too, because the ladies at bingo and bowling paid attention to me. I felt like I was part of something. At her oil painting classes, I became part of the clan. I'd go around and look at everyone's projects. I got them the things they asked for and asked questions about the different color blends or what type of brush they used to get the different effects.

One evening, when Mom and I arrived, the ladies had taken up a small collection and purchased me a canvas, some paints, and a few brushes. No one had ever done anything like that for me. I was overcome with emotion and started to cry. I couldn't believe they had thought about me outside of the class and bought me these art supplies. Someone saw ME! To my surprise, even though I felt I had no talent for oil painting, I got an honorable mention when I entered one of my paintings in an art show. It was such an exciting time in my life!

My mother's depression came across in varied ways. Although I could not see it as a child, I can now. She would take a two-hour nap each day. I knew better than to disturb her. If I had, she would have blown up at me and threatened to tell my father, which was never good. She would disassociate herself from us like we didn't exist. She would tell us to go outside and play and not come back in until she told us to... sometimes six or seven hours would pass. My father was at work and didn't know what was happening.

We learned how to make our own lunches because we didn't get fed unless she was hungry. I tried to stay ahead by packing snacks or a small lunch and taking off for the day. I'd go to Presquile Park and ride my bike through the trails or build a fire in one of the BBQ pits and roast wieners. I had babysitting money after age 11, so I would sometimes pick up food at the grocery store and stash it in my room. I'd also see if my friend Nadine or Lisa were home and hang out at their place for the day.

My mother was not interested in doing housework, so the task befell us. Inspection of our work was a familiar ritual. If it did not meet her expectations, we had to do it again, and we'd be given another job on top of the first one. Perfection became a way of life. Be quiet; play outside; clean the bathroom; don't fuss; eat everything on your plate; shovel the sidewalk; get good grades; … all these things, done to perfection, or risk seeing that look of disappointment, which usually leads to unbearable consequences.

I wrote a poem at the age of 13, and with a teacher's help, it was published in an Autism magazine. I should have been very excited about having this poem published, but I wasn't able to share this excitement with my parents. It seemed that every time I got good marks in school, my dad would say to my other siblings, "Why can't you guys get good grades like Joanne," or "You need to apply yourself better," or "If one of you's don't come home with straight A's like Joanne, I'm going to wup all of you's". As a result of this kind of 'praise,' my siblings hated me. They teased me and called me names like 'smarty pants,' 'brown noser,' and 'daddy's favorite.' I often got left out of games. I felt like an outcast. They would often lure me to play with them, and then once I took the bait, they would ridicule me and push me away.

I remember in grade eight, we had an English class where we read a short story and then answered three to four comprehension questions on the back of the card. The reading program was called SRA. The structured system helped learners develop independent reading skills, fluency, and confidence. It was set up like an index file where each new level was a different color…red, green, maroon, brown, and so forth.

I loved to read and liked the questions on the back of the card. I was usually finished before anyone else in the class, so, out of boredom, I worked ahead and managed to do two or three stories per period. I had them stacked up inside my desk and just reached in each day and handed the next one in the series to my teacher. I had enough assignments stored up to last till the end of the year by February.

My teacher caught me going into my stash one day. He told me he wanted me to meet with him and the principal the next day to discuss the matter. I was petrified. I'd never been to the principal's office before and wasn't even sure what I did wrong. When I got to the principal's office that next day, they said, "What are we going to do with you, Joanne? You have four months left in the school year and have already finished the year's English curriculum.

Upon further examination, we have discovered that you have almost finished the math book exercises. This is what we are proposing: We would like to know if you would like to become a classroom tutor and help students who are struggling or behind in their school work. If you still want to be challenged, we can assign you some grade nine curriculum you can work on at home at your own pace. We want to talk to your parents to inform them of the changes".

Although I was pleased with myself that I wasn't in trouble and was excited to work ahead at a grade-nine level, I began to cry in the office. Both my teacher and the principal looked shocked at my reaction. When they asked me why I was so upset, I explained the following: I told them that my dad would brag about my accomplishments to my siblings, and I would be teased, outcast, and even physically bullied. I told them that I did not want to stand out in any way. I practically begged them not to tell my parents. To my amazement, they agreed. So, no one was the wiser at home, and my low-key existence continued.

There were times, however, when I actually admired my mother. She had days where she was not isolating, and I could watch her do things that amazed me. She would take a picture from a drawing contest and replicate that picture with so much finesse that you couldn't tell the difference between her drawing and the one in the magazine. She never entered the contests, but she enjoyed the challenge of the activity. Sometimes, she would draw cartoon pictures for us. Sometimes, I'd watch her play solitaire to be in her presence. I didn't care that I could only watch if I were quiet.

When we were younger, she made clothes for our Barbies. It was tedious work putting snaps and little zippers on pantsuits and dresses, but she seemed to enjoy getting lost in the activity. She also enjoyed gardening. My siblings weren't interested in gardening, but I saw it as an opportunity to get close to her. I'd follow her around and ask a million questions. She'd tell me the names of the different plants and flowers, and I'd help her pull weeds.

My mom was also involved in the horticultural club, which ran out of our high school. I often entered different flowers at the shows and enjoyed looking at the displays. My mom would cook a roast beef dinner each Sunday, with Yorkshire pudding and mashed potatoes. We even got a small sherry glass full of my dad's homemade wine. One year, we picked dandelions all day till we were yellow up to our elbows so he could make his dandelion wine. I would help my mom cook, and it became my job to make the gravy each Sunday and set the table for six.

I figured out that I had to become interested in what she was doing to get her attention. I'd say I got very good at certain things as a matter of emotional survival. I tried to insert myself into her life as much as possible. Sometimes, she'd let me in, and sometimes, she wouldn't. I learned to defend her when perhaps she didn't deserve to be defended, simply because I was trying to preserve the times. I remembered feeling somewhat connected with her.

As an adult, I became curious about how this 'love thing' really worked. And so, I loved my own children differently. I tried to mirror images I learned by watching other people with their kids. At times, it felt uncomfortable to embrace my own children, but I knew how important it was for them to feel loved. It didn't come naturally to me. It was a conscious effort and a challenge I embodied. The payoff was astronomical….they loved me back!! They were teaching me how to love.

After having experienced what love actually felt like, the last interaction with my mother, although 22 years in the making, was plausible. This interaction occurred due to a phone message left on my spouse's phone while we were traveling on the west coast of Canada.

We had stayed at Miette Hot Springs, 61 km east of Jasper, in the Canadian Rockies. We had no cell reception while staying at this resort, and as we came down the winding dirt road to the main highway, my spouse's phone messages slowly started to come through. I played the messages back through the speaker in our rental car. One of the messages was from a man with a very thick English accent. My spouse asked me who it was. It was my father! I had not heard his voice in 22 years, and it felt very haunting to me to hear it now. The message stated that my mother was in the hospital and did not have long to live. We were due to return home from our trip in two days. I couldn't wait to get back.

For years, my father pushed all of us kids away so he could have my mom all to himself. I thought, here was my chance to see my mom without him around to intervene. I needed closure.

When I returned home, I went to the hospital every day for two weeks until her passing in October 2015. She did not recognize me; sometimes, she thought I was one of her sisters. I just played along so as not to confuse her. My mother was dying of kidney cancer, which was complicated by Alzheimer's. During those two weeks, I read to her. I brought in her favorite butterscotch pudding cups. I also brought her most beloved house plant to place on her window sill…an African Violet. I was with my mother just hours before she passed away. I had my peace with her. I began to realize what unconditional love really was.

After reading the book on mothers and after having internalized the messages from the book I needed to hear, I wrote the following poem: 'My Mother Who Couldn't Love Me.'

September 21, 2021
My Mother Who Couldn't Love Me

To my mother, who couldn't love me
I bare no animosity
As a child, it stripped me of emotion
But as an adult, charged my curiosity
I was quiet and kept all of your secrets
I had to insert myself into your day
Otherwise, I'd have served you no purpose
And you'd never have met me halfway
You spent days in a state of depression
I felt unwanted, unloved and neglected
I tried to reach through it and find you
But my attempts to get through were rejected
I was known as the silent observer
Watching other family dynamics play out
While keeping a comfortable distance
And protecting my psyche, no doubt
I emerged somewhat timid but stronger
Your legacy will not be passed on
The cycle for which I was destined
The mistrust and abandonment gone
My determination to be a better parent
Drove me to be so much more
I now have two beautiful children
Whom I unconditionally love and adore

It felt like a transformation had taken place after reading this book on mothers. I saw that by fighting my own instincts of uncomfortable physical interaction, making a conscious effort to embrace my own children had really paid off in the long run.

I am not lost in the delusion that my children did not genuinely feel my forced efforts. As adults, they seem hesitant at times, and I can see this hesitation on their faces. I can hear it in their voices. They are treading lightly, not knowing how much to give or what to expect in return. It's difficult for me to convey. Although it is uncomfortable for me to show affection, I am bursting with love inside for them and want them to feel that love. I'm doing my best and hoping it's enough.

JOANNE SMITH

"I am no bird; and no net ensnares me: I am a free human being with an independent will."

Jane Eyre

SEVEN

Diamonds Are Created Under Pressure

THE JOURNEY WITHIN

"I can't think of any better representation of beauty than someone who is unafraid to be herself."
Emma Stone

They always say the bigger the stress, the better the outcome. I truly believe that!!! There was a point where I completely gave up on myself and my future.

Feeling helpless and not in control of my own life and my financial situation was enough for me to say enough is enough. I say how my future plays out, and I will be on the court taking that next shot.

2019 was a tough year. I just recently moved back to Vancouver, British Columbia, and I was trying to get back on my feet and get business going. I knew I wanted to make people feel good and look good from the inside out. And I had this strong desire to put my beauty schooling and courses to use.

I had just gone through some trauma. I had lost a baby, my landlord sold the house, and there was mold. I was quite sick from the mold poisoning from living there, and I was quite sick. During that time, I received a call from one of my best friends, Heidy and Simi. They said I should come and stay at their house. They told me they got me while I got back on my feet. I'll never forget the conversation in Toronto with Heidy when she said to come home to Vancouver.

I didn't hesitate! I got in my car, sold everything, and drove back to Vancouver across the county for the fifth time. Some trips I did alone over 4500 kilometers with me and my dog, Mylo, who passed away a few years back at 17 years old. I have driven from Vancouver to Toronto a total of six times now.

As I was driving into the city, I had chills, reliving what I went through. I left in 2014. I lost my condo I bought at 24, my clothing store, and the clothing company I had built. I had dealt with a lot of trauma and left Vancouver in a hurry to save my life and had not returned since. It was a bone-chilling feeling coming over me. I filled up with tears. I was finally home again. I had to face the fears that took my power away. I was a shell of a person.

To this day, I'm grateful for that phone call and for coming back, dealing with, and overcoming that one moment that took my life away for over eight years.

My mom, Judi, moved away to Alberta in 2004 to be close to my grandmother Dorothy and reconnect with her family after moving to British Columbia in her early years. I'm a born and raised West Coast girl all day long. I absolutely love nature and water and the mountains. I feel connected to the earth and nature. It's the one thing that grounds me.

Mom always mentioned how she missed BC and regretted selling her home in Alberta. However, she was there for our family and her Mother Dorothy. After my grandmother had passed, Mom's connection was here with me. I invited her to come back to BC to live together and told her not to worry; we'd figure it out.

After living in Toronto for seven years and going through my healing and growth, I was back in my hometown, facing my fears, but the one thing missing was my Mom. I had been staying with Heidy and Simi for about six months and working towards getting our own place.

I had reconnected with an old friend who had just built a beautiful home with a brand new three bedroom basement. It was the perfect opportunity to get a place for us all to share expenses and rebuild our lives.

Soon after that, Mom was on her way to Vancouver!!! I was pretty excited. We had not lived in the same city for many years. I would be lucky to see my mom once a year, if not every few years. It was time for us to spend quality time together again.

Imagine being raised as an only child and being away from the closest thing to family you have. Toronto to Alberta isn't just a quick drive. I enjoyed flying and spending Christmas with Mom and the family, but it wasn't enough. All we have is the time we have left.

Just a few months into Mom living in BC, we had the opportunity to rent the other unit inside this huge home and convert the two bedroom, one bathroom into our own business and Salon.

My Mom, Judi, had been a hair dresser since before I was born, and I have some experience in the beauty industry. I do permanent makeup and lash lift and tint. It was a perfect time to create a family business together.

We had our business license approved and started putting all the equipment together. We even had two full pedicure chairs and hired movers to move them and bring them inside. Tons of expenses gathering tools, equipment, time, and effort were put into this business.

We started having a few other women working with us as well. One was a nail tech, hair, massage, acupuncture, and a lash tech. Things were starting to get going, and a few customers were coming through our doors, and then the pandemic hit!

What a slap on the face! I was broken into a million pieces: all the money invested and the energy. I literally gave up. I cried for weeks.

Doors shut. No income is coming in. No more clients, period. I thought this was a chance to get back on my feet established in Vancouver. A chance to work and create an income and business alongside momma Judi.

I came up with a referral stamp card when we had just opened. Refer three new clients and get my next service free. It was a way for clients to earn free services and ways to get new customers in the door, not just for myself but for the rest of the ladies working with us.

The income dried up when the doors were shut because of the pandemic. We were devastated, along with the rest of the families and businesses. There had to be another way to continue referring to each other customers for their services and not be in the same place or city. A huge lightbulb went off!!!!!

I will share a back story of How Our Beauty Squad & Lifestyle Referral Network Vision came to light in 2019 and where we have evolved.

One thing I am absolutely grateful for is the Network Marketing and Direct Sales industry. The skills and training were top-tier. I have gained skills and confidence in multiple companies over the years. I absolutely love the industry and what it has given me in mindset mentorship, motivation, and team building.

I have seen certain things occur in past companies, such as compensation. I always asked myself why they changed the compensation plan. The company rebrands or switches formulations and, even worse, gets shut down! I have seen families' incomes completely cut off without warning.

The simple answer is EGO and GREED, not truly caring about the people and cutting corners. They forgot what it was like being in the trenches with us working to make a commission. Training teams of people worldwide, building an army to sell their products, and get new members. As we all know, duplication and retention are the keys to any business!! So why cut off the hard-working people's incomes and livelihoods? We should lift people from the bottom up and create opportunities for others.

The ones working daily present their company in the field, busting their butt to make money for their family—the hard-working person to pay bills or put a roof over their head. Day and night, they were presenting the business and the lavish lifestyle. They were the ones who made it to the top. Unfortunately, in most cases, painting a false sense of reality for most who will quit before they make it. Or better yet, CEOs buy private jets, fancy cars, and homes, with family over-riding the entire organization to cash in. I have seen enough to cringe, and we wonder why the MLM, or direct sales industry, has been given a horrible reputation 😬.

The family puts their last $500.00 in with the hopes and dreams of creating income to support their children. That's who gets hurt—a false sense of reality and being fed a dream rather than the honest, hard truth. The struggle of what it takes to make it in the industry should be told.

The ones who struggled or didn't Fast Start right away or Rank up were left to fend for themselves. I don't know how many uplines have left me to figure it out alone. Enough to make most quit or give up and get a job; some had internal struggles, or something else came up.

The key in business is to help people earn the money they invested back as soon as possible or gain value from the initial investment. If you support and teach people how to make a paycheck or stand behind a cause, you will have them for life. I'm not saying that as a sales person or giving business advice. I'm saying it's reciprocated when you add value to a person's life and family as a member of the collective community. Unfortunately, this is not always the case. Not all Owners or leaders are created equal.

You ask what this has to do with Our Beauty Squad & Our Lifestyle Referral Network. I promise it's getting there...

They say entrepreneurship is a roller coaster, and I have been on a wild ride for the past decade. From dealing with health issues to inadequate website developers, breaking through has been a constant struggle. I have had more people sabotage rather than truly support. And it comes with Entrepreneurship. Not everyone is authentic. You really truly grow in the process of finding your tribe!

They say that you only truly value what you earn. The true gain is from the process you grow and the lessons learned. This company truly saved my life.

All during Covid, I was so depressed I wasn't sure what to do with my life. How was I going to earn income? Dealing with a major neck injury and spinal injury and considering having surgery. I was in no financial place to decide to take time off from launching this company. I have no backup plan or security. I'm fighting for my life and vision, one day at a time. With everything I have left in me! I must launch this company no matter what pain I am in.

When the company becomes a mission to serve others, it's not about what you're personally going through anymore. You block out your struggles, and you keep fighting no matter what.

I have gained so much strength in the process. Yes, I have felt lost, failed, lost money, invested and lost everything, started businesses, and failed. It's the knowledge in the process you gain every single time you fail. Think of each road block you overcome as a learning lesson and how you could do it better the next time.

You eventually get to a place where you find another way, no matter what it is. The only limitations you have are the ones you set for yourself.

With all of the experience over the years that I have gained in the direct selling and MLM industry, I decided to create a company and community that was truly for serving others.

I'm here to show you that anything is possible if you believe in yourself. Don't be afraid to chase your dreams, even when things get tough.

There were times when I felt like I had no one by my side and moments when I wanted to give up. But each one of those moments taught me something important. They taught me how to be resilient, they showed me how strong I am, and, most importantly, they reminded me why I'm doing this.

My dream isn't just about running a successful business; it's about creating something that will last, making a difference, and showing that dreams, regardless of their size, are definitely worth pursuing.

Ladies, listen up! Your dreams matter. Your drive to succeed is valid. Don't let anyone tell you that it's not possible. Own, cultivate, and have confidence in yourself, even when the world is against you.

Be the legacy of that amazing woman who never gave up on herself and her dreams. It's not only about creating a successful business; it is about inspiring others to follow their passions and never give up on their dreams, no matter what. We can be true visionaries to each other and for generations of women to come!

CALLI JENSEN

"She was free in her wildness. She was a wanderess, a drop of free water. She belonged to no man and to no city."

Roman Payne

EIGHT

Tears Into Triumph

COACHING SOULS TO FORGIVE AND FLOURISH

"I am the blood of the dragon. I must be strong. I must have fire in my
eyes when I face them, not tears."
George R.R. Martin

Empowered, Personal Journey.

We will discover the beauty and power of embracing our authentic
selves. I've pondered the word anxiety and how we get triggered.
When I was growing up, we never heard these words. I remember
feeling confused and anxious, like a deer looking into a car's head-
lights. Then I sat with this.

What came to me was when I was little.

I came from domestic violence abuse. One memory that lives inside is
my parents fighting and screaming at two o'clock in the morning. I
would run out of the house, thinking of it now. I don't even know
how I got outside.

My mom and I would hide under a tree. To give you a backstory. My
dad was six foot 10! He was a giant to everyone, but he was really big
to me. Mum is five foot two.

So, under the tree, we would wait, afraid to breathe. What if the tree branches moved? In silence, we waited and waited. Then, when we thought it was safe from being (the tree runners), we laughed about that when I was older. It was time to go inside the house. We lived on two and a half acres, and at the back was a basement door. Funny thinking of it now.

The door squeaked. Why my mother never put oil on it, I never will know. I learned to be very quiet, shallow breathing as I opened the door, in very small movements so as not to make a sound not to wake the giant my father. We had a dog, So I also had not to get her to bark if we made noise. Once inside, I had to close the door silently. Yahoo, we made it by now; who knows what time it is?

Sleep was needed. But as a little girl, it was like being with one eye open and being very sensitive to the environment. The fear and adrenaline ran through my body. I was always a high-energy kid. I wondered why. Then I realized the adrenaline had been running through my body since childhood. I've lived in this state for years. It became normal for me to feel this way. It got higher and higher. It was a drug to me. But I didn't realize it.

My hypersensitivity put me above anxiety, and this is where I lived. So, when people talk about anxiety, I couldn't relate. Exploring these two words, anxiety, and hypersensitivity, showed me the chemicals running with flight or fight.

Visualize a sprawling tree with deep roots firmly planted in the ground. Each branch represents a generation burdened by anxiety, passed down from one to another. As we explore the intricate network of these roots, we uncover the hidden stories, experiences, and beliefs that have shaped our anxious tendencies. We can begin to untangle ourselves from their grip by understanding the origins.

How did I get here? Oh, my time has flown by. I look back and see my life in sections. Living in the moment, it passed by. Being in the moment and seeing what kind of play I have written. I can't make this shit up. I look at each loving soul as a character in a play. It makes life way more fun. What is at the table today? What adventure shall I have? Who will I love? Who will drive me crazy or piss me off? Then, I take a moment and look at what feelings I have.

Is it sadness or anger? Disappointment or joy. Did I buy into it? Is it charged with emotion? There's the gift. When I'm conscious of that moment, everything changes. It's like a gateway to strength, embracing vulnerability. Imagine a delicate butterfly emerging from its cocoon.

Vulnerability is our cocoon.

Protecting us from the inside and the outside world but also preventing us from truly experiencing life's wonders. As we learn to embrace vulnerability, we unlock a reservoir of strength within ourselves.

Envisioning a community coming together, extending their hands in support and compassion, we find solace, strength, and the belief that we are not alone on this journey.

I have run into people I went to school with, and now I am not afraid to talk about the abuse and how I lived. I then heard stories that my little child inside dealt with, and I wasn't alone. We were all going through the same thing. Domestic abuse and violence. What was normal that we lived as children? I didn't know what I would think was better. It was just really different abuse.

Looking back again, in time, I lived beside a family that had four kids. I was always going over there. I never wanted to be at home. I guess I knew my home was not safe.

How do I know that now? Well, I had a mom who would lose her shit.

She was like a single parent. Dad worked away six weeks at a time, thank God. Mum came from Wales and was an only child raised by her grandmother because her mum died when she was about six months old. Grandpa was a womanizer.

In my early childhood, besides my dad doing his behavior when he came home, my mom would throw shit at me. From beer bottles, pop bottles, plastic phones, knives, whatever she got her hands on.

Are we seeing a pattern? Yep, fear.

I also had the famous basement where you could run around in a circle. A dear friend of my Mum told me a story.

One day I got my Mum so mad. To my surprise, she had a broken beer bottle. What the fuck? It all happened in front of her friend with her child. She shared how it scared both of them as she tried to calm my mom down. Well, she must have calmed her down. I didn't get hit with it.

But the point of this is people witnessed this. It was traumatizing for them, too.

So the big question is: Was that a safe environment? Hmm, no. So now you know why I ran to the neighbors that was safer? Or was it?

As a child, we need love to be held and cared for. So, that little angel would experience inappropriate touch and sexual abuse. The fellow was four or five years older and a teenager. I would be involved in the behavior for years. What love is? Sexual touches? Hiding the secret became the thrill.

What does that sound like? Yeah, the chemical high. I want you to understand whatever the sexual stuff was or the violence. It's about what it did to my beliefs. My body high.

No price can be paid for this. It was set in stone. I didn't choose my beliefs. My body locked them in.

I moved at age 12 and a half. I was so upset that my 'drug supplier' would be cut off, but not really. He could drive now.

So it continued once in a while. The new home you would hope to be a new start, yeah, not. I had a knife thrown at me and hit my bedroom door. So, just before 16, I made my mind up: I'm out of here. I needed to have my driver's license, as my mom had to sign it. So I got it, and I moved out.

Awakening from the Shadows

In the dimly lit room, anxiety and fear cast long shadows over the person's face, stifling their dreams and ambitions. But within this darkness, there's a glimmer of hope, a cascade of light that pierces through the gloom, illuminating the path to empowerment and freedom. This journey of self-discovery and transformation begins with exploring anxiety's depths and the revelation of the dormant power within.

A Moment of Clarity

I vividly recall a moment from my past that would shape my understanding of self. I was about to enter my parents' home, where I often felt an inexplicable shift in myself. It was as though, upon crossing that threshold, I would step into a role, a character that wasn't truly me. The details of those moments elude me, but the feeling remains etched in my memory.

Walking into that house, it was as if I had donned a mask, playing a part scripted by their expectations and desires. Yet, as soon as I stepped outside, away from those confines, it was like emerging from a spell. I'd wonder, "What just happened?" I returned to being the person I recognized, the one I was before entering that house. This curious experience led me to see life as a grand stage where we all take on roles for each other, often unaware of the profound influence of resonance and entrainment.

The Dance of Personal Power

As I reflect on my life's journey, I can see how I, as a child, unknowingly surrendered my power. I became a paradoxical mix of a control freak and a free spirit to regain control and safety. I craved adventure, from jumping out of planes to walking on fire, lying on beds of nails, and scuba diving. These experiences, I believed, were about shattering limiting beliefs, but in retrospect, I understand the allure of the adrenaline rush.

My love for adventure extended beyond the physical realm. When I traveled, I rarely planned beyond one or two nights at my destination. The thrill came from the unknown, the unpredictability. It was like living in a constant state of excitement.

The Power of Perception

The documentary "What the Bleep Do We Know" profoundly impacted my perspective on life. It all boils down to our thoughts and the chemicals coursing through our bodies. Nothing inherently carries meaning; the meaning we assign shapes our reality.

As I look back on my life, I can't help but chuckle at my younger self's drama-queen tendencies. Thankfully, we didn't have ubiquitous video recording back then! In my early twenties, I played a quirky game I dubbed "Spencer Darts," involving quarters and butt cheeks – a strange, albeit hilarious, party trick.

The Dance of Perception

But as I recount these events, I realize that nothing possesses intrinsic meaning in life. Consider this: If I were to say something offensive to a stranger on the street, their reaction would reflect their own internal world, not a judgment of my worth. What emotions did I trigger in them? What was transpiring within them? My words were merely a catalyst, revealing their own internal landscape.

In life's grand drama, we have a choice: to buy into the narratives that unfold around us or to observe them with detachment. If emotions well up within us, it's a sign that the story has touched something within our hearts.

Life Happens for You, Not to You

Remember, life is not happening to you; it's happening for you. This perspective shift, inspired by the wisdom of Tony Robbins, is the key to our journey of self-discovery and empowerment. The shadows of anxiety may loom large, but they also conceal the radiant light within. In the coming paragraphs, we will explore this inner illumination and learn to wield it as our greatest strength.

Moments Beyond the Veil: A Journey of Astonishing Encounters

When I was just a wide-eyed 19-year-old, I went into a bar named Champagnes. My intention? To catch a glimpse of some male strippers, of all things! Little did I know that night would lead me down a path of surreal experiences that would shape my understanding of life.

As the night unfolded, these strippers donned characters from fairy tales like Hazel, Gretel, and even Humpty Dumpty. They weren't just performers but magicians, conjuring laughter and excitement from the crowd. Their professionalism was awe-inspiring.

But what happened in the periphery of that smoky bar would forever imprint itself upon my memory. As I stared at the stage, something inexplicable occurred. Time ceased to flow. I kid you not; it stopped right then and there.

My gaze was locked on that stage, and suddenly, it lit up like an amusement park at night. It was as if the universe had decided to grant me a sneak peek behind the curtain of reality. In sheer astonishment, I turned my head to the left, and time stood still once more. The world outside that glowing stage froze in its tracks.

Not one to dismiss such extraordinary occurrences, I turned my head to the right. To my amazement, time suspended itself yet again. It was as though I had a taste of the divine, a glimpse of a realm beyond our own.

When I finally returned my gaze to the stage, everything came alive again, and I found myself sipping on a humble glass of orange juice. "What's going on?" I wondered. Little did I know, this was just the beginning of my journey into the enigmatic world of spiritual experiences.

Years later, I would understand that I had brushed against the supernatural on that fateful night. It was a revelation, a stark reminder that our body is but a vessel, a mere "meat suit" for the soul within.

Life took another intriguing twist when a woman walked into my world, bearing her own tale of the inexplicable. She recounted an evening at a friend's home where she spoke of her beloved dog. Strangely, the dog disappeared from the house, only to be locked inside a car outside, with no logical explanation. Who could have possibly moved the dog?

Then, her astonishing journey from Vancouver to Abbotsford in British Columbia should have taken an hour. She called her brother to announce her arrival, only to find herself at his doorstep 15 minutes later. They stared at each other, flabbergasted. She whispered, "Like, wow," as she realized she must have traversed some temporal wormhole.

These stories are just the tip of the iceberg in my collection of bewildering encounters. They serve as my compass, guiding me through the labyrinthine mysteries of life. They've taught me that logic and reason do not explain everything neatly.

One particular memory lingers vividly in my mind. While with WFG Insurance, I entered a room through an open door. In that fleeting moment, I became one with the room itself. I had no body, no physical form. It was a sensation both bizarre and electrifying.

But as quickly as it happened, I thought, "Where is my body?" Instantly, I was yanked back into my corporeal self, like a rubber band snapping back into place. The shock left me speechless, struggling to find words to describe an experience that transcended the boundaries of ordinary existence.

These moments have shown me that life is far more mysterious and magical than we often dare to imagine. They've taught me to embrace the inexplicable, to roll with the cosmic tides that sweep us along on this wondrous journey. In the end, these extraordinary moments remind us of the boundless depths of our existence.

Life is a whimsical journey filled with unexpected twists and turns. Sometimes, the most magical moments happen when we least expect them, like the night I met Mark in the 1990s. It was a time when cell phones were bricks and adventures were waiting just around the corner.

One evening, I found myself at the Irish Rovers pub, ready to dance the night away with my friend Christine. She wore a flowing skirt, and the pub was packed. We managed to find a lone seat, so she sat like the princess she was. I chose to stand.

As I stood there, a tap on my shoulder signaled that a seat had opened on the other side of the table. It was a serendipitous moment. Laughter filled the air as we and newfound friends Mark and Dean embarked on an unforgettable night in Vancouver. Little did I know that this was just the beginning of an incredible adventure that would take us from Vancouver to Langley and beyond.

But what made that night so special, you might ask? Looking back, I believe it was the beginning of a powerful journey that would teach me to harness the power of thought and visualization. At that time, I secretly began to write about the kind, adventurous, and loving man who had just entered my life - Mark.

It wasn't just about love, though. I had other dreams, too. I scribbled on a piece of paper that I wanted a Porsche, a 944. What happened next was nothing short of remarkable.

Weeks later, Dean called me, asking what I was doing for New Year's Eve. My friend Betty and I were planning to go dancing at the Ocean Beach Hotel. Dean and Mark decided to join us, and they drove up to pick us up in my car. As I gazed out the window, I couldn't believe my eyes. My dream car was pulling into the driveway. It felt like a sign, a playful wink from the universe.

The surprises didn't end there. Mark and I decided to embark on a trip to Cancun, Mexico, as friends - a respectful choice at the time. The goal was to explore the caves 33 feet below the surface. We enrolled in scuba diving lessons, and I was excited about diving into crystal-clear waters.

But when I descended just 10 feet, something changed. The vastness of the open ocean overwhelmed me, and fear took hold. I had to surface, and tears streamed down my face. I must have seemed crazy to Mark, but I couldn't push past that fear.

Back in Canada, I made a decision - I couldn't let fear hold me back. I needed to face it head-on. That's when I found George in Port Coquitlam, an instructor who understood my apprehensions. He let me progress at my own pace, even if that meant taking baby steps.

For those unfamiliar with the process, getting a diving license meant taking a test in an SFU pool. The test involved putting on a mask, a regulator, and flippers, and then diving 33 feet to the pool's bottom. It was a daunting challenge and an opportunity to confront my fears.

As I descended to the pool's depths, something magical happened. I watched my own bubbles rise through the clear water as if I were watching a movie. I was frozen in time, observing myself as I performed each step of the dive. Taking the regulator out of my mouth, exhaling bubbles, and then inhaling again - it all happened with a sense of ease and grace.

Finally, I surfaced, and an exhilarating bolt of energy shot through me. I was on a high for days, and it wasn't just adrenaline. I had conquered my fear and learned to trust life in a way I had never thought possible.

The journey was far from over. Australia's Great Barrier Reef and the waters of Cuba beckoned, promising more adventures and discoveries. My story is about love, courage, and the incredible power within us when we dare to chase our dreams and face our fears.

Join me as we dive into destiny, one chapter at a time.

JULIA HIK

"She has fought many wars, most internal. The ones that you battle alone, for this, she is remarkable. She is a survivor."

Nikki Rowe

NINE

A Shattered Heart

A MOTHER'S DESCENT INTO DARKNESS AND HER
JOURNEY BACK TO LIGHT AND LIFE

"Faith sees the invisible, believes the unbelievable,
and receives the impossible."
Corrie Ten Boom

I'm dedicating this chapter to the men, women, and children who have suffered the inflictions of sexual abuse, domestic abuse, addictions, negligence, and any other wounds. It was a wound I thought could never be healed. It damaged my worth as a person, and I believed it was my fault.

You are not alone for the men, women, and children whose abuse was perpetrated by a loved one. For the men, women, and children whose wounds were inflicted by their fathers and mothers, I am here to tell you that there is a God, and He is the father to the fatherless, and we are made perfect in His image, and he sees us as flawless, He can and will provide for your every need, and He will fulfill his purpose for you in this world and turn your pain for good.

I was born in 1976 on a small farm outside of Airdrie, Alberta, and am the youngest of four children. Growing up, I used to think I had an amazing family and upbringing. The normal to me was living in a house of addictions, violence, alcoholism, emotional, psychological, mental, and emotional abuse. I am grateful that God protected my heart during most of my youth, and the deeper memories of abuse didn't surface until my late 30s after my second divorce from an abusive marriage.

My mom was a Christian, and my dad grew up Catholic before turning from God when his dad was killed in a construction accident when he was 18. Both my parents immigrated from Europe. My dad is from France, and my mom is from Scotland. My dad is deceased, and my mom is about to celebrate her 80th Birthday. I still miss and love my dad to this day despite the abuse and trauma endured through their addictions.

My dad, at 18, had to take responsibility for caring for his sister and mother after his father died, and his bitterness and resentment towards God carried on in his life. Although he was a Catholic, I recall him telling me he turned his back to God and only really remember him talking about the devil and Satan as anything.

I didn't grow up with any real spiritual teaching and first recall entering a church for a funeral for one of my friends in grade seven. My dad often had outrageous bursts of violent anger, usually alcohol in the mix, and abuse perpetrated against my mom. I recall this from my earliest memories, being afraid for my mother's life often. The screaming, objects thrown, some of my pets hurt in front of me, leather belts, soap washes in our mouths, vulgarity, etc., etc.

I recall, at a young age my mom leaving my dad to go to her sisters in Ontario, and we were left home alone with my dad.

These displays of what I thought was normal and love led me into three abusive marriages, and enduring similar abuse all over again time and time again. As a child, I accepted this as love, and how would I have ever known better?

I never recall a normal, vulnerable conversation with my mom as she too was always in trauma and addictions. There were no "I love you's," no hugs, and no displays of love beyond what finances could buy. I never felt heard or seen by anyone growing up.

As a child, I had dreams. I dreamt of being a Veterinarian or Olympic gymnast and a mother to have children to love the way I never had been. Many of my dreams were never met as my path would be one of abuse and addictions. I still grieve those losses today but pray God can use me for a bigger purpose.

I know I'm not alone. I have met many other women with stories more horrific than my own and am grateful I've been spared in many ways. It was a truth that shattered me on every level, and I work daily to forgive.

On June 20, 2002, one of my dreams came true, and I gave birth to my daughter, I remember holding her for the first time, looking into her eyes, and thinking God must be real to give me such an amazing gift.

My son was born on December 8, 2003, and was not under anesthetic, so I met him immediately at birth. He had these little blue eyes and a scrunched-up happy newborn face and my family was complete, another blessing from God.

I was blessed to be able to stay home with my children for the first five years, before returning to work. I became a personal trainer at that time and had a home business turned storefront.

Working out had become a passion for me as my kid's dad worked out of town, and being in a women-only gym with childcare allowed me time to make friends and get some adult time with other moms, while still being close to my kids.

What I didn't realize was the gym would pull me into the competition world and into the downfall of a lot of my health, the lack of self-worth, and the inability to stand up for myself.

With my kid's dad working out of town and my own business, my marriage was strained. The distance, infidelity, abuse, and addictions destroyed our marriage. My ability to be healthy and have the tools to forgive did not help.

After my divorce, I continued to run my CrossFit business, was a nutritionist and trainer, volunteered weekly in both my children's classrooms, attended church, managed their hockey teams, and raised my kids alone. Their dad began threatening me, telling me he was going to take our children from me. He had a new girlfriend with a child, and either couldn't or didn't want to pay support.

I was alone, overworked, and afraid of the anger and threats. It was around that time that my childhood abuse memories began to resurface.

A yoga instructor at my work invited me to a bible study, and in 2012, I surrendered my life to God. I believed that all would be easy. Most Christians know that there is a real war between good and evil in this life, and that began the war for my soul.

I started counseling that year to address the abuse as a child finally. I confronted my dad and told my family. My sister said she could not walk the journey with me. I lost my entire family, my children, my business, my home, my car, and my finances in a year. I lost a sister whom I thought was my best friend.

Alone, in fear, and afraid for myself, and into the darkest pit.

I know this may be hard to read and hear, but I have forgiven and know many children endure far worse and I am grateful for my life. A leather belt hung on the knob outside my door, and if we spoke without being asked or I ever tried to tell my truth, it would be abuse. The beginning of being silenced began, as I saw no use in fighting for myself. If I tried to tell about any abuse, I had my pants pulled down and beaten in front of my siblings.

I spent most of my youth alone in my room, writing in my journals…..hoping someday someone would find me and see me, hear me, love me, and help me.

By age 12 or 13, I was smoking, drinking, sexually active and pregnant. My mom read my journal and found out. She forced me to have an abortion and made me promise never to tell my dad. I was forced into two more abortions by age 19.

After I shared with my family about my abuse, I was committed to a mental hospital, my brother threatened to sue me if I ever spoke about it, and that's when I decided I would never be threatened again. It has taken me over ten years to share my story.

On May 7, 2013, my children's father's lawyer would in a moment illegally serve me the evening before the court with an affidavit accusing me of starving my children, not taking them to school, and beating them along with 37 other points.

My family who supports my ex took my children from me, and their finances disabled my ability to fight in court to see my children.

For seven years though I had joint custody, but I never saw my son or daughter.

The court battle included false kidnapping allegations which resulted in police enforcing no-contact orders with my children. I went from being a full-time mom to childless. It is a wound I am still trying to overcome.

The loss of my kids sent me down the most horrific path into a relationship with a cocaine addict. I nearly lost my life to after having my head held underwater until I couldn't breathe. My boyfriend at the time got me into cocaine. The addiction helped me to cope with the emotional pain of having my children taken from me.

I used cocaine, marijuana, heroin, crack, alcohol, and MDM and became an escort, sold cars, and worked 22 hours a day for six months. I sold my body for money for lawyers. I was homeless multiple times and in and out of jail for trying to see my kids. A simple wave and I love you at the school landed me in the remand center. I was driving past my daughter, coincidentally, and again, I'm in jail. My family's way of getting back at me about finally speaking up initially by supporting my ex-husband.

I was then able to retain one of the top lawyers in the city, to order the first of two four-year-long bilateral assessments.

I was able to see my daughter once on November 24, 2014, and I still remember and appreciate that moment to this day.

Unfortunately, this first order resulted in the therapist quitting when my children's father refused to pick up the Christmas gifts, she had asked for her and her brother that I had purchased for them.

I realize now God used prostitutes in the bible to display his redemption, and I am not ashamed. I feel for all the women I met who turned to the same thing. There is a love so deep for a child that a mother would go to any depth for her children. I thought, If Jesus died for me, I can do this for them, and for the justice they too deserved.

No child should be kept from a mother when she is clean living, and that's exactly what happened before I spiraled down with the loss.

Neither my family, nor my children's stepmother or father showed me any mercy in fact, spent a huge some of money to make sure I never had a chance to see them or speak to them. I set up five different homes for them, had many friends and support was accountable for years, and showed the courts for them over and over again.

The thing is...the truth always comes out. Eventually, children grow up and realize right and wrong.

I have seen and experienced a lot of corruption in the police and court systems and realize this injustice is real.

It is unfortunate that in family court, a person can go in with false allegations and have children taken away. I know their father was kept from his mother, and so repeated the pattern due to his lack of education and counseling.

I still firmly believe I am 100% anointed to be my children's mother, and that no man can separate God's will for my family.

After the court assessment, my family and kids' dad said there had never been any abuse in our family and home. I had a major relapse with cocaine and went to my kid's home to tell them I loved them. The family vehicle was there, but no one answered. I went to the back door and broke it down to see my kids. They weren't there, and I went to prison. This was one of many times I would attend a jail on the no contact breeches because I desperately wanted to see my children and not even the courts would help me after years of sobriety.

I was diagnosed with complex PTSD in 2014 and again in 2017 after four years without my children. I prayed and fasted and felt a nudge to move to Okotoks. I took a job at a clinic whose owner belonged to a church in High River and whose front desk girl was the daughter of a women's ministry home for women recovering from abuse.

It was definitely God who led me there. I was able to stay in the home and get more counseling, and doctor care. I was again diagnosed with CPTSD. I attended hour after hour of counseling, went through another two-year bilateral assessment, and finally, the assessor apologized to me for not believing me about the childhood abuse. I had so many women help me and pray for me and believe in me, and still so grateful for them.

The court ordered for the second time reunification therapy, and this time again it was thwarted by allegations from the other side of collusion.

I went back into a depression and contemplated again giving up on my life and signing over custody.

On March 19, 2019, I prayed to God for a husband, as I had stayed alone just hoping for reunification with my kids.

It was the next day I met my current husband. He too had abuse as a child and I didn't realize had nearly a lifelong steroid addiction he had kept hidden. We got married right away as we both believed God had brought us together for that purpose. I was still hoping for my kids and asked him to get rid of his steroids, which he did, but not before taking most of what he had left. I had never been around these before and didn't realize the rage that would ensue and sexual aggression.

I leave most of this story out for his privacy, but I reached my end of enduring the abuse caused by the substances, and though I don't believe in divorce, nor believe it is God's will, filed for one. After divorce filings and an EPO, I was able to attend Saffron Center for more counseling and more EMDR. I am free from all prescription medications, and all substances, as is he just recently having overcome a 35-year steroid addiction.

I never wanted a divorce; I just wanted the abuse and addictions to stop. I prayed to God to give me a sign, as I hoped by some miracle, he could stop the divorce. It was one of those tiny, hopefully, but still doubting prayers.

At the last minute, our divorce got rejected by the court, and I was able to see the root of his addictions and decide to try one more time and forgive again. I am happy he now has the opportunity, and he is starting at the Saffron Center as well for his childhood abuse.

We have fought for each other, not always in the right ways, but with a good heart. God has given me and my family so many second chances, and I am grateful for these. I have always chosen to never give up on the people I love as was done to me so many times. I am grateful for the strength God has given me, the endurance to keep going, and truly his divine intervention that has saved me so many times.

All of these things are what brought me to my knees and to God, and in the last few years, I have seen God answer so many prayers, even the silent tiny ones hidden in my heart that I thought he could never hear or see.

He has brought so many people into my life that I am so grateful for.

I prayed and journaled for my kids for five years when I had no way to talk to them, which gave me some reprieve from the pain.

There is something so horrible about wearing shame when that is not God's design for us, and I have met so many people who have carried their trauma and shame of such abuse without having an opportunity to open up.

I have rejected every label, unkind and untrue word spoken over me, every diagnosis given, and dug to the root of my trauma, believing in God's unfailing love and belief in his healing. I have chosen to believe in what God says about me and who He is continuing to read the bible and keep those words as my own.

One of my favorite verses is Jeremiah 29:11, that He has a plan for a good future for me, and Proverbs 3:5-6 To trust in the Lord with all your heart and not lean on your own human understanding. I know His love never fails, and He can turn all meant for evil into good in my life.

Since becoming an RMT, I have tried to pray for all my clients and their healing, and I believe massage therapy is an amazing integral therapy in treating addictions and trauma stored in the body.

My son did come home in 2020 after seven years, and I am so grateful. I can't explain how it felt to see him again after so many years. Surreal, I could literally feel and know he was going to come home days before he did and told my husband we needed to set up the spare room. I have been able to spend a lot of time with him, repairing the relationship, and it was the most precious day to finally see him, hug him, and be his mom again.

Not a day goes by that I don't thank God for him and his life. I didn't know I could ever love someone so much, and we have shared so many special times together, he is the kindest, most caring, courageous, and strongest young man, and I am so honored and proud to be his mother.

I know my upbringing impacted my ability to be a good parent and inflicted wounds on my own children as well, and I strive daily to be the best mom I can be.

I have yet to be reunited with my daughter and miss her every day, and pray that day comes soon. I also am looking forward to meeting my stepdaughter, and believe after my husband's counseling that can happen.

It's a daily choice to choose love over hate, forgiveness over bitterness, and see myself as God does. Pure, holy, and redeemed.

I believe God will use my story and life to help other women, men, and children who have suffered through abuse.

I am praying for my husband's healing and that our daughters can also see what a life not given up on can do and how any story can be used for God's glory.

I am so grateful for my husband, who never let me quit pursuing a relationship with my kids and fought for me in so many ways to keep going.

Forgiveness is a constant continuous choice that I have many days had to force myself to make.

I know God can take away the shame and guilt carried by people who have endured abuse, and His mercy and Grace are unfailing. He has taught me to forgive, and through many stories in the bible, that He does protect His people, and through the power of prayer, there is nothing he can not do.

I am God's and always will be...

I hope to one day start a charity and family protection home not just for women but for their children and as well the whole family in cases of abuse. I'd also like to have a center for wholeness with massage, therapists, holistic therapies, doctors, lawyers, and all that families need to overcome addictions and be healed from the wounds from their past.

He has taught me how to forgive what seems unforgivable.

God has proved himself to me over and over again through so many different circumstances and has increased my faith.

I continue to thank Him and ask for my life to be an example of His healing, so I can help others.

I will continue to fight in prayer against any evil or sickness in my family and for our protection.

I am grateful for this life and believe we are to be beacons of light to others in darkness. I refuse to allow what has been done to me to diminish my light, and I pray for all the women, men, and children who have suffered abuse to find the peace of Jesus and his healing love and restoration.

I have forgiven all who have hurt me and choose to let love win.

NICOLE SARAH DUPONT-SCOTT

"Stop telling girls they can be anything they want when they grow up. I think it's a mistake. Not because they can't, but because it would have never occurred to them that they couldn't."

Sarah Silverman

TEN

Heather's Tree

A LIFETIME OF TRAINING

"Now therefore go, and I will be with your mouth and teach you what
you shall speak."
Exodus 4:12 ESV

The story of Moses serves as a timeless narrative that reflects the universal themes of personal growth, self-discovery, purpose, and the resilience of the human spirit. It teaches us that, like Moses, we all have the potential to embrace our unique paths, confront challenges, and find our own "Promised Land" of fulfillment and purpose.

Self-discovery and personal growth require a journey that I, too, embarked upon, just as Moses and countless others have throughout history. This journey was and still is marked by the challenges and trials of life itself.

My path led me to become a life coach, a guide for others on their quests for self-discovery and fulfillment. You, too, can discover your unique purpose/s and become the living embodiment of your own aspirations and dreams.

In this chapter, I invite you to journey with me through the trials, challenges, and revelations that led me to this path. As you read my story, consider your own journey — the humble beginnings that held the potential within you waiting to be unlocked and the unique trials and circumstances that have shaped your life until now.

People may encounter the same circumstances, but what we glean from those encounters is as different and as vast as there are people. If you were to line up seven people to observe the same circumstances, each person would have a different take on what happened. This is why police officers need to get as much information from as many people as possible to piece together how an actual event occurred.

Even identical twins born within a few minutes of each other, raised in the same circumstances, by the same parents, etc., still do not have the same perspective. They can even pretend to be each other very convincingly, but something always separates the two. With that in mind, we are all destined to do different things, to be unique, and in my thoughts, not only for the benefit of ourselves but also for the greater good.

Everyone's life journey is challenged at some time or other in all the same areas. These areas are physical health, mental health, finances, careers and education, relationships, and spirituality. These challenges are all opportunities to learn about ourselves and about others. Challenges in each of these arenas, in conjunction with education, mentorship, trial and error, and skills practice, take us to the fulfillment of our potential. They are the stones on our path, the raw material from which we sculpt our unique masterpieces. Just as a sculptor's chisel shapes a block of marble into a magnificent work of art, these challenges, and the tools we use to navigate them mold us into our best selves.

Moses' journey begins with humble origins. Born into a Hebrew family during a time of great oppression, he is placed in a basket and set adrift in the Nile River to escape the Pharaoh's decree to kill all Hebrew male infants. Everyone begins their journey feeling vulnerable and uncertain, not knowing where life's circumstances can lead; they can be harsh and unpredictable.

By the grace of God, I was not born into such a harrowing existence. My beginnings were humble enough, though. Born into an average family of equal Scottish and Canadian heritage, I am the third child of three. However, I was acutely aware of the disadvantages some of my peers experienced.

I was out on the school playground at recess when a friend asked me if they could talk to me alone. We found an old cedar tree at the back of the playground, and there we sat, talking about the difficulties my friend was having with her mom and dad. I was all but seven years old at the time. It was here that I learned how to listen, to be discreet, and how not to gossip.

From that day forward, whenever I sat in the tree at recess or lunch, students I knew and those I did not would come to me individually to talk over their problems. That old cedar tree became known as "Heather's Tree." If someone needed to talk, I was there. Otherwise, I was on the playground like all the other kids.

I was particularly impressed by the wide girth the kids would give the tree if I were talking with someone; it's as if they just knew to keep their distance so as not to disturb us or eavesdrop. Even the teachers kept their distance ~ I'm not sure they knew what was happening!

As long as I remained at that school for another five years, "Heather's Tree" was in operation.

Through these formative years, I learned a great deal about myself and my abilities by participating in such organizations as Girl Guides and through various sports, martial arts, and a particularly nasty piano teacher. I learned discipline, about my ability to survive out of doors, and lost and gained confidence.

Moses' life takes a significant turn when he is adopted into the very family that vowed to eliminate him. Here, Moses is mentored with an education befitting royalty, the best of everything bestowed upon him.

Mentorship can come in many forms, not always in an official capacity nor in a positive setting. I can safely say that I have had and still have a lot of mentors in my lifetime, whether they or I knew that at the time. I can now look back and see how much influence people actually had in my life that brought me to where I am now.

Not all mentors are "warm, soft, and fuzzy."

I worked as a bar manager in a semi-private golf club. When I wasn't in the bar, I was under the watchful eye of a general manager who didn't like my "hands-off style of management" when it came to managing the other staff. I would tend to give someone a job to do and let them do it; as long as the job was completed on time and well, what did it matter how it came about?

She would talk about me to the other staff members within earshot and would "tell me off" in front of the staff. She would literally make up scenarios to be sure there was something she could embarrass me about. Eventually, to her joy and to my relief, I was let go. I recognize that she lacked self-confidence in her abilities and that all she had to say about me was not about my performance. It reflected how she felt about herself.

I've learned and continue to learn valuable lessons from my family members. Having children taught me that throwing a temper tantrum, especially as an adult, just escalates the situation, essentially getting you nowhere quickly.

My son continues to mentor me by listening to his unique perspective on things. My daughter exemplifies compassion, patience, and the ability to forgive. My husband has shown me unconditional love and that humor proves to be a valuable tool in keeping the peace and enjoying each other.

By far, my most significant mentor has been Christ Jesus. The Bible speaks about how one should conduct oneself physically, mentally, emotionally, spiritually, and ethically, and Jesus embodies that conduct. His example and His teachings are profound: a way of life, not a bunch of rules to follow. My desire has been to emulate Him, to show the mercy and compassion He has, to extend grace in all circumstances, not to judge, to forgive, and to love unconditionally.

Mentors have shown me what works and what doesn't work. They have given me wisdom, accountability, skills for improving emotional intelligence and communication, encouragement, challenges, and insight into the way people conduct themselves and why they do what they do.

Friends tend to be tactical in how they deliver mentorship.

"Do you know what you do?" queried my friend.

"Do I know what I do? I do payroll, pick up and deliver parts and employees …" I began.

"No, no! No no! Do you know what you DO?" interrupted my friend.

"Umm, I'm not sure what you mean," I answered.

"You're a life coach!"

"I'm a what??!!"

That was the first of three very similar, independent conversations I had with friends within a few days!

Hearing something from one person is interesting. Hearing the same thing from two might be worth a little more effort to look into. However, when you hear the same thing from three close friends, completely independent of each other, it's time to take notice.

What the heck is a Life Coach?

"a person who counsels and encourages clients on matters having to do with careers or personal challenges." Oxford Language Dictionary

I must admit, that definition explained to a "t" what I was already doing!

Physically, I was extremely active in sports and life. I loved time in nature as well as with people. I was a competitive swimmer in high school and dove headfirst into underwater hockey for the Canadian National Women's and Mixed teams at University.

I canoed, cycled, hiked, climbed, and snorkeled. I've been spelunking, cliff diving, and horseback riding. I've embraced martial arts and scuba diving, and competitively played every sport imaginable except lacrosse and hockey (I was always the goalie in pick-up hockey games as no one was able to lift the puck and I was always on the ground ... my team won a lot). In my later years, I participated in Obstacle Course Races and continue to participate in an annual cycle challenge to raise money for Kids' Cancer (the Great Cycle Challenge Canada, www.greatcyclechallenge.ca).

Competitive sports taught me about punctuality and time management, discipline, resilience, teamwork, perseverance, adaptability, accountability, and relationship and communication skills. I learned about sportsmanship, that failure is just as important as success, and that celebrating other peoples' success is a necessity.

I sometimes think I should have been a cat, given my ability to survive so many misadventures; I must be on my ninth life! I've had broken bones, head injuries, twisted, sprained, and wrenched tendons and ligaments, a torn kneecap, pulled muscles, and have been sporting scoliosis from birth (my spine's way of keeping me in line). I've had all the typical burns, scrapes, bruises, and whiplash, all for the sake of adventure, and the signs of the misuse of my body have come to fruition. I now understand the significant importance of self-care.

I also received training from more structured or official sources.

At University, I began my studies in nutrition and realized that I was more interested in understanding how people think, why and how people make decisions, and how to change behaviors. I graduated with a Bachelor of Arts Degree in Psychology and continued my passion through my love of books. I regularly consume such authors as Brene Brown, Darren Hardy, Daniel Goleman, Malcolm Gladwell, Daniel Kahneman, Dietrich Bonhoeffer, Steven Covey, Brendan Burchard, Dallas Willard, and many, many others who speak to the human condition.

The decision to become certified as a Professional Life Coach was a natural progression, and graduated from Fowler International Academy. I was also offered the opportunity to become one of a handful of Certified Disaster Recovery Coaches.

Since I was so passionate about helping others, I jumped on the opportunity as it would allow me to be called, at a moment's notice, to go anywhere in the world where there was a natural or unnatural disaster and help people figure out what to do with their lives, now that they no longer have a place to live or work.

Training comes from several sources, each creating a specific learning atmosphere. Even within a particular industry, sport, art, etc., the composition of training varies as widely as the individuals themselves. My training began at the young age of seven and has never stopped.

In grade 7, I went to another school as the school boundary lines had changed, and I was around different students. I knew a few of the students but had to navigate my new circumstances and find new friends. It quickly became evident to other students that I was discreet, a good listener, had a wealth of knowledge, and had the ability to convey that knowledge in an understandable and usable way from all of my years of practice. I never advertised, yet again, another place was found for my mentorship.

I got my first "real" job at the age of 13 as a pool change room attendant. This was my introduction to being non-judgmental as I took from and returned some interesting belongings and noted how untidy and irresponsible people could be at any age.

In High school, I became a lifeguard, swimming instructor, and eventually pool supervisor in several of the city-owned indoor and outdoor pools. I was elected as my class representative for the student and athletic councils every year. I joined the choir, the high school band, and the swim team, participated in a number of sports clubs and school plays and was recognized for my leadership in sports, student services, and academic achievement in my last three years. I was surprised and humbled by the public acknowledgment and learned to accept praise with humbleness and gratitude.

Again, I never advertised, and yet the lunch room, the parking lot, or wherever there was a private spot was fair game for my mentorship. In that same high school, a young man aspiring to be a detective wanted to prepare a dossier on me, but to his chagrin, no one would say anything about me ~ I was well protected!

Moses' life takes another profound turn when he encounters a burning bush that is not consumed by the flames. In this encounter, he is called by God to lead the Israelites out of slavery in Egypt. Each person has the potential to receive a "call" or revelation that awakens their sense of purpose and responsibility in the world. However, Moses is initially reluctant to accept this calling, showing his true feelings of self-doubt and hesitation when faced with life's challenges. Yet, he embarks on a journey of self-discovery, facing trials and tests along the way. This journey is akin to the personal growth and self-exploration we undertake to understand our unique strengths and weaknesses.

University and College found me in many leadership roles, although I was, in reality, terribly "shy" (I suppose introverted is descriptive enough). My self-confidence was never very strong, so I really wasn't interested in being a leader, but I could no more say "no" to these positions than stop breathing. No matter where I went, I was given a leadership role. I'm sure I was thrust into leadership roles in which I probably had no business. Each role provided the teaching of its own unique skills and talents despite my initial trepidation.

My leadership roles at work continued as I was forever organizing trips and special events for my coworkers. Once my kids were of age, I was a Sparks, Brownies, Guides, and Pathfinder leader for my daughter and assistant soccer coach for my son. Chair of this, and chair of that …. My advice always seemed to be needed.

People whom I didn't know would just open up and tell me their life stories wherever I went and then invited comments. In fact, some insisted on my comments, which, although honest, were not always well received. However, over time, they understood and thanked me for my frankness, explaining that they wished they'd listened to me.

Throughout Moses' leadership, he encountered numerous obstacles and hardships, including the resistance of Pharaoh, the trials in the wilderness, and the rebellion of the Israelites. Life is filled with adversity, and personal growth often requires facing and overcoming these difficulties. He evolves from a reluctant leader to a strong and resilient figure. This transformation represents the capacity for personal growth and development that lies within each of us as we learn from our experiences and rise to the occasion.

Being a reluctant leader comes with its own unique difficulties, as you continually face opposition from those who desire your role or wish to pursue their own methods. This was my opportunity to hone my relationship and communication skills and gain resilience.

Moses' legacy endures through the ages as a source of inspiration and guidance for those on their own journeys, reminding us that our actions and choices can leave a lasting impact and contribute to the greater good.

Over the past 57 years, I have probably had more opportunities and exceeded the recommended 10,000 hours of intentional training ("Outliers: The Story of Success" by Malcolm Gladwell); however, I am constantly learning new and exciting things. The more I learn, the more I realize I don't know. With that in mind, I would hardly call myself a master, knowledgeable and helpful, but perhaps not a master, particularly in my ever-changing field. Events and circumstances continue to shape the coach I am.

Moses' ultimate purpose was to lead the Israelites to the Promised Land, a place of freedom and fulfillment. As human beings, we are on a quest to find meaning and purpose in life, to seek a "Promised Land" that represents personal fulfillment and contentment.

I was never one to hang around with other girls much. Most of my friends were boys. I thought girls were mean, catty, gossipy, and annoying. At least with boys, you knew where you stood. They'd get mad, duke it out, and get it over with. Girls held grudges for years, talked behind your back, treated you one way, and thought and talked about you another.

And yet here I am, a life coach for women and loving it.

I love helping people, especially with life issues. Women supporting women, empowering them to be the best they can be and fulfill their purposes at all stages of life. For women to manage their lives without losing themselves or burning out in the process.

As you can see, "Heather's Tree" followed me wherever I went. It wasn't always a "tree," but that is where it all began. Now "Heather's Tree" is in my home or wherever I choose.

Come and sit for a moment in Heather's Tree:

As I reflect on my journey from that old cedar tree on the school playground to becoming a life coach for women, I'm reminded of the power of resilience, growth, and embracing unexpected opportunities. Life often leads us down unexpected paths, and sometimes, our true calling emerges when we least expect it.

I want to leave you with this thought: You, too, have the potential to make a meaningful difference in the lives of others and to discover your own unique purpose/s. Embrace your passions, overcome challenges with determination, and never underestimate your impact on those around you.

Just as 'Heather's Tree' followed me throughout my life, offering a safe space for others to open up and share, know that your own journey is filled with opportunities to create positive change. No matter what you're considering as a career or if you're simply seeking to make a difference in your own way, remember that your experiences, talents, and insights are valuable.

You have the ability to empower, inspire, and uplift those you encounter on your path. Embrace your potential, nurture your passions, and continue growing, knowing that the world is better when we share our gifts with others.

So, step into your own 'tree,' your unique sphere of influence, and let your light shine. The world is waiting for your positive impact, and together, we can create a brighter, more empowered future for all.

HEATHER O'REILLY

"One by one she slew her fears, and then planted a flower garden over their graves."

John Mark Green

PART II
Meet the Contributors

THE WARRIORS BEHIND THE WHISPERS

Please take a moment to appreciate the warriors who shared their stories within these pages.

These women have overcome their own personal challenges and now share their inspiring journeys with the world. Courageous and brave, as you can imagine it is not easy to share a chapter of your life story.

These warrior women it to bring light on the issues many women in our world face. To stop generational trauma and to step up and shout, "ENOUGH."

This is your chance to learn a little more about these remarkable women and their journeys. These profiles are vivid snapshots that capture the very essence of courage, determination, and inner strength.

Each author has her own unique story, with her own set of challenges and victories. They have each chosen to be vulnerable and share a small piece of themselves with you.

It is a privilege and honor to introduce you to these incredible women who have persevered and emerged as beacons of hope for others.

Let their truths inspire you on your own journey.

"Everything is within your power,
and your power is within you."

Janice Trachtman

KAY BOHEMIER

ESCAPING A CONVICTED KILLER

ONE SURVIVOR'S HARROWING TALE

Kay Bohemier, was born and raised in Manitoba, Canada. She is a proud mother to four awesome kids. She has been very blessed in her life, both personally and professionally, and thanks God for every new day given to her.

Kay tackled University in her 30s and graduated in the field of Local Government. She moved on after mastering that role and got my commercial license. Kay has thoroughly enjoyed the challenges in her new field.

Kay is a huge advocate for domestic violence and has spent time volunteering for a domestic violence program, helping others navigate through the system to obtain help and make safety plans.

Her goal is to start a non-profit organization and build transitional communities for survivors of domestic violence—homes where survivors and their children don't have to worry about a 90-day stay. Kay says she will continue to fight for changes in domestic laws and seek accountability for those in power.

Kay wants to help others find their voice; together, we CAN AND WILL make a difference.

If you would like to reach out to Kay, you can do that here:

kaywood95@gmail.com

Kay can be found on YouTube here:

https://youtube.com/@kaybohemier7553

News articles Kay would like to share with you:

https://www.wsoctv.com/news/local/convicted-killer-spend-decade-prison-robberies-3-local-counties/LFAOGBRXNJAMNLVXCDXX47OWB4/

https://www.lincolntimesnews.com/news/suspect-charged-in-death-of-man-found-at-denver-home-fire/article_b53d424d-114b-5c81-a60f-133c9f7eca8d.html

https://www.cbc.ca/news/canada/edmonton/kay-bohemier-john-paul-gaddy-prison-domestic-violence-1.5595601

https://www.wsoctv.com/news/local/i-felt-like-hostage-local-woman-shares-story-marriage-convicted-killer/Q6REGJBHZVH2ZGKCPP232FEGJA/

JILL FISCHER

A SINGLE MOM'S UN-HYPNOTIZING JOURNEY

DANCING WITH QUANTUM EFFICIENCY INTO FREEDOM

Jill Fischer is an Energy Healer, Hypnotherapist, Coach, and International Teacher. She is the Founder and President of the College of Holistic Healing and has a Masters in Energy Psychology and Clinical Hypnotherapy.

Jill works with people who struggle with chronic illness, weight, relationship issues, grief, stress, and anxiety. With her unique deep healing process, she helps people feel healthier, calmer, lighter, and happier than they've ever felt before so that they can live a more fulfilling life. Over the past 15 years, Jill has supported thousands of people to transform their lives.

After a long history of pleasing other people, Jill reclaimed and took charge of her life and created a multiple six-figure healing business while raising two healthy children as a single mom.

In addition, Jill has had tremendous success as an international artist and teacher of graphic design. She co-hosted a renowned national TV show in Japan teaching English.

Her mission is to promote holistic healing so everyone can experience optimal health and live a joy, love, and laughter-filled life.

Jill is graciously offering her Free Self Worth Meditation at the Beach to support you in aligning with how amazing, brilliant, and beautiful you are. www.selfworth.online

If you're struggling with your health, weight, relationships, or life direction, click here to connect with Jill for a free I Love My Life Discovery Session. www.jillfischercall.online

If you want to know more, I'd love to support and guide you back to your natural state of abundance, health and fulfillment.

Jill Fischer

Life Coach, Hypnotherapist & Energy Healer

Unlimited Energy Class: www.energy-health.online

Meditation: www.selfworth.online

College: www.chh.online

Connect: www.bookwithjill.com

KATHERINE WELLS

THE WILL TO LIVE

A LIFE STORY OF RESILIENCE

Katherine Wells was Born in Surrey, British Columbia, Canada in 1991.

She is a survivor of MCFD (Ministry of Children and Family Development) with First Nations ancestry and grew up in the foster care system. She is a trauma survivor and has overcome a lot of grief in her lifetime — Many experiences and many stories to tell.

Throughout all of this she has remained strong, she has a heart for other people, and she has not let these experiences define her. She likes to spend her time with family and friends, she loves drinking coffee, laughing, nature and listening to music.

Katherine is currently living in British Columbia, Canada, with her son. She has been a mother for nine years.

She battles with severe fibromyalgia, and has other health complications. Her life has left her with some emotional scars to heal as well.

She is currently doing EMDR (Eye Movement Desensitization and Reprocessing) and learning to manage her chronic illness.

She has not given up hope for the future, and she is happy to be a part of this movement. In hoping that her story will reach those who need to read it.

LISA HUPPEE

THE DESIRE TO DO BETTER

WHY CAN'T IT HAPPEN?

Lisa Huppée is the owner of six 'Just Like Family Home Care' franchise locations throughout the Lower Mainland and Vancouver Island of British Columbia. Lisa's journey has been challenging, but she believes resilience is the key to accomplishing great things.

Just Like Family Home Care has provided her with opportunities to connect people of all ages and backgrounds to assist them in the home care they need, Lisa has always been compassionate, and finding work that connects her to this side of herself has completely changed Lisa's life.

Lisa's recent accomplishments, receiving local community awards for her services, reminded her that finding a deeper connection to our work can make a difference.

At Just Like Family Home Care, they offer in-home assessments to match clients to a staff member that fits their individual needs.

Finding the right fit for each client is vital, as personalized care and support set Lisa's business apart from other home care providers.

Helping families balance their commitments and family life inspires her to continue to build her business.

Lisa's past work life as a teacher helped her to recognize the importance of personalized care when preparing student IEPs. Just as each student has unique challenges, each individual needing home care has a personalized care plan to help them and their families plan for success.

Her early life wasn't easy; she doesn't think she could have ever expected to be where she is today.

Lisa grew up on the prairies in a small town in Alberta. She was shy, reserved, and self-conscious. But was dedicated to her school work and committed to figure skating.

This is where Lisa learned the value of hard work and determination and that nothing comes easy in life. Self-reflection daily, weekly, and yearly helps her see if she is challenged and doing good in the world. Being accountable for her actions is what helps Lisa stay on track, both as a person and in her beliefs and goals.

Fast forward to today, Lisa is living a very different life. She is a business owner. She has had time for her hobbies, painting acrylics and watercolors, meditating, and expanding her spiritual interests.

Lisa now has the freedom to travel when she wants to, a supportive and loving husband of nearly ten years, and the puppy pack that she has always dreamed of.

Today, Lisa is living the life she has always desired, in the mountains, but near civilization, with the people and pups she loves.

She knows that life changes can feel unattainable, but she's writing her story to share that it can happen once you put your mind to accomplishing things!

https://fraservalleybc.justlikefamily.ca

https://westvancouver.justlikefamily.ca/

https://www.justlikefamily.ca/locations/british-columbia/tricities-pitt-meadows-maple-ridge

https://richmonddeltabc.justlikefamily.ca/

HANNAH THURIER

WILL THIS PAIN EVER GO AWAY?

I THOUGHT MY PAST DESTROYED ME, IT ONLY GAVE ME STRENGTH

Hannah Thurier is a 34-year-old Anishinabe Ikwe from Pinay-mootang First Nation, Manitoba, Canada, located on the land of Treaty 2 Territory.

Hannah comes from the Woodhouse Family, a family name that is written in Indigenous historical archives. She is a direct descendant and 5th generation to the original 1871 Treaty 2 signatory, Chief Richard Woodhouse.

Becoming a published author in the Women like me book series has been a great blessing for Hannah, and she says it has been a 'life-changing' experience.

Hannah never thought that experiencing something so traumatic would have such a unique transformation in her life. Being able to accomplish something so extraordinary has ignited a creative side of her that she never knew existed.

Implementing podcasts and literacy is Hannah's new life journey. It has unconsciously had her manifesting a desire to tell her story.

Hannah enjoys helping others and has always been one to lend a helping hand. This characteristic trait of hers has helped Hannah in previous work endeavors and with friends and family.

While writing her first book, she put on her 'writer's cap,' wanting her audience to read her story through her eyes and understand that even though she was seen, she wasn't Hannah and to understand, and her feelings were never considered. She has longed for that, but this writing experience helped her correct her thinking and reminded her to prioritize herself, listen to her heart, and love herself.

Hannah wants her audience to smile at the end of her story and be happy for her. For them to send positive vibes her way and say to themselves, "You go, girl!" Each reader having that moment at the end of Hannah's story will come her way and pave the way to a prosperous life, not in person but through their love vibes.

If you'd like to reach out to Hannah, you can do that here: h.thurier@hotmail.com

JOANNE SMITH

MY MOTHER WHO COULDN'T LOVE ME

MENDING THE BOND THAT WAS NEVER THERE

Joanne Smith has recently enrolled in a Holistic Nutritional Counselling Course. With this recent endeavor, she is now embarking on a mission to help herself and others improve their health.

Joanne has a Developmental Service Worker diploma and has taken courses from the University of Waterloo in Psychology, Behavior Science and Kinesiology.

She is active in her community, attending a local gym three days a week, yoga classes, joined a walking club, plays pickleball at her local sports centre, attends a Writers Collective meeting twice monthly and runs a home-based business.

Joanne is currently in the process of publishing her first book, an autobiography/healing/thought-provoking look at overcoming personal trauma. Joanne has taken this self-discovery approach, alongside psychotherapy, to build new pathways to who she wants to be and to share her opportunities for personal growth.

She has two grown children and lives in a small community in Ontario, Canada. She enjoys hiking, cycling, sewing, puzzles and reading.

Joanne can be reached at activelady07@hotmail.com.

CALLIE JENSEN

DIAMONDS ARE CREATED UNDER PRESSURE

THE JOURNEY WITHIN

Ms. Jensen is an incredibly dynamic West Coast Vancouver lady. She has a deep, profound love for people, animals, life, and the great outdoors. She loves serving and empowering people as she lives her dream life.

Ms. Jensen is known by many for her love for life and living it large. Over the years, she has chosen many industries such as Entertainment, Promotions, Events, Networking, Beauty, Fashion, Health & Wellness, and Sales to live her fun, enjoyable, passionate life.

Due to what she personally went through and witnessing first hand how many were affected adversely by the pandemic, she took ACTION. She Founded the Largest Online Referral Network the planet has ever experienced. Today, she continues to live her purpose and passions as she continues to enjoy her life while making a difference for others globally.

Over the years, Ms. Jensen has done a lot of community work with giving back in many ways. She has been invited to be a part of and even formed Women's Empowerment groups. Ms. Jensen has helped

ıd men globally to step up to reclaim their individual-
, power, and identity in their own lives. For this, she has
y acknowledged and featured in various publications and
ıd awards for her outstanding contribution to others.

ould like to reach out to Calli Jensen, here are a few ways you
ıd her:

w.ourbeautysquad.com

ıttps://www.facebook.com/groups/ourbeautysquad/

JULIA HIK

TEARS INTO TRIUMPH

COACHING SOULS TO FORGIVE AND FLOURISH

By embracing our authentic selves and facing challenging circumstances, we discover our true selves by acknowledging our path and confronting our fears.

The long-lasting impact of childhood trauma and the ways in which it shapes our beliefs and behaviors. It serves as a reminder that many people carry hidden scars from their early experiences.

The relationship between hypersensitivity and anxiety highlights how heightened awareness can lead to chronic anxiety. It helps us understand that anxiety isn't always an isolated issue but can be deeply rooted in one's life experiences.

Embracing vulnerability, we discover inner strength and resilience.

Julia hopes you will question the meanings we attach to events and understand that our thoughts influence our experiences. She encourages you to be open to the mysteries of life and embrace the extraordinary experiences that can shape our understanding of the world.

Julia believes in the power of our dreams and visualization in manifesting one's desires. Demonstrating in your life with intention and believing in the possibility of achieving them can lead to remarkable outcomes.

Our past doesn't define us, and with self-awareness, courage, and the embrace of vulnerability, we can find our true selves and uncover the strength within us to face life's challenges and chase our dreams. Julia encourages you to believe in the power of transformation and the magic of life's unexpected moments.

If you are curious about releasing old patterns and generational trauma. Julia invites you to have a heart-to-heart chat with her.

She offers NLP, Hypnosis, and Biofeedback.

If you'd like a complimentary copy of 'Journey of Self Awareness' pdf book, please contact Julia at the email below.

"May you feel my love from my heart to yours".

coachjuleshik@gmail.com

www.juliahik.ca

NICOLE SARAH DUPONT-SCOTT

A SHATTERED HEART

A MOTHER'S DESCENT INTO DARKNESS AND HER JOURNEY BACK TO LIGHT AND LIFE

Is a believer, wife, and mother of three.

Nicole has a diploma in business as well as massage therapy and recently became a licensed insurance agent. She has owned several business, including a cleaning company, personal training studio, CrossFit gym, and currently runs a mobile massage therapy business in and around Edmonton, Alberta.

She is a two time figure pro card winner, CrossFit games regional team qualifier, and multiple 5k sprint winner. She enjoys time with her husband and children. She enjoys health and the outdoors, mountain hikes and river walks.

Nicole hopes to help and inspire men women and children with her story and is passionate about helping people and fighting for love, justice, and forgiveness and all that God is. She has a strong will and faith and believes in never giving up on the people she loves.

If you would like to reach out to Nicole, you can do that here: nicole-scott1752@gmail.com

HEATHER O'REILLY

HEATHER'S TREE

A LIFETIME OF TRAINING

Heather has coached and mentored individuals and facilitated small groups for over 40 years. She is a certified Professional Life Coach and Disaster Recovery Coach.

Her mission is to empower women to be who they were made to be without losing themselves in the process.

She is a strong proponent of walking the walk and talking the talk. When something works, she loves to pass it on to others!

Here are a few ways to reach out to Heather:

Free consultation: https://bit.ly/3DI0g0F

Email: heatherlynnecoach@gmail.com

Cell/Text: 613-561-7146

Web: www.heatherlynnecoaching.com

Weekly newsletter subscription: https://bit.ly/3KigksP

"She was tired of everyone deciding her life for her. She was ready to figure out who she really was--not what anyone else told her to be."

Marissa Meyer

PART III
About Women Like Me

"My scars teach me that I am stronger
than what caused them."

Manal al-Sharif

Women Like Me Community

The power of women's stories lies in their ability to inspire, challenge, educate, and connect. They are both a reflection of individual experiences and a testament to collective strength. In sharing and honoring women's stories, we can recognize the contributions, challenges, and diversity of women's lives.

Empowerment Through Unity - One voice can make a sound, but a chorus can shake the earth. "Women Like Me" is more than just a movement; it's a collective voice of women from different walks of life coming together to make meaningful changes in society. By joining, you amplify that voice and make it resonate even louder.

Shared Experiences - No matter our backgrounds, women around the world face similar challenges. By joining this movement, you get access to a wealth of shared experiences and insights that can inspire and guide you in your personal journey.

A Safe and Supportive Space - The "Women Like Me" movement offers a platform where your voice is not just heard but celebrated. It's a space where you can express yourself without fear of judgment and where your experiences are validated.

Opportunities for Growth - Beyond sharing stories, this movement provides personal and professional growth opportunities. Members can access resources to help them thrive in their chosen paths through networking, workshops, mentorship programs, and more.

Making a Difference - The stories in the "Women Like Me book series" aren't just narratives; they serve a larger purpose. By supporting this movement, you directly contribute to empowering women to care for their families.

Celebrate Womanhood - At its core, the "Women Like Me" movement is a celebration of being a woman. It's an embrace of our strengths, vulnerabilities, stories, and potential.

In essence, joining the "Women Like Me" movement is more than just aligning with a cause; it's a declaration. It says you believe in the power of women, in shared stories, and in a future where every woman has the opportunity to shine. Will you lend your voice, your strength, and your passion to this vibrant tapestry of womanhood?

Join Us Here:

https://www.facebook.com/groups/879482909307802

"Beautiful creatures cannot be confined.
Her wings will grow, she'll find the sky."

Christy Ann Martine

Women Like Me Book Series

Everyone has a story. And oftentimes, those stories can be powerful things that help us learn and grow. But for some people, their stories can be a source of pain. They may feel like they can't escape their past or that their story is holding them back from living their best lives.

If you're one of those people, know that you're not alone. And more importantly, know that there is hope. There are ways to turn your personal story into something positive and to find healing from the past.

One way is to share your story with others. This can be incredibly cathartic, and it can also help others who have been through similar experiences. you process your feelings and work through any trauma you may be carrying around. And finally, don't forget that your story doesn't define you. You are more than your history. You are more than your pain. You are more than your mistakes. You are more than your story. You are strong, you are brave, and you are enough. So don't let your story hold you back.

Writing about your past can be very beneficial, both emotionally and psychologically. You can increase your feelings of well-being and even improve your physical health. When you write about your past experiences, you relive them in your mind. This can help you to process difficult or traumatic events, and it can also provide you with some closure.

Additionally, writing about your past can help you to understand yourself better and work through any unresolved issues. It can also allow you to see yourself in a new light, which can be both healing and empowering. In addition to helping you emotionally, writing about your past can also be beneficial physically. Studies have shown that expressive writing can help to reduce stress, anxiety, and depression. It can also help to improve your immune system function and promote a sense of calm. So, if you're feeling stressed out or overwhelmed, consider picking up a pen and starting to write.

We only have one shot at this life, and it's our only shot. There are no do overs. There are no second chances. So, we better make the most of it. We only have this moment right here, right now, and it's the only moment that matters. We only have so much time on this planet and must spend it wisely. We only have so much energy and want to spend it on things that bring us joy. We only have so much love to give and want to give it to people who appreciate it.

A story is a powerful thing. It can draw you in, take you on a journey, and leave you with a lasting impression. That's why I love listening to other people's stories. Everyone has a story to tell, and I'm always eager to hear a new one.

Visit the Women Like Me Stories website at:

www.womelikemestories.com and get in touch. The world will be waiting.

Women Like Me Stories

https://womenlikemestories.com/tell-your-story/

"I have forgiven all who have hurt me
and choose to let love win.
She is thunderstorm with a touch of lightening."

Eman

Julie Fairhurst

"I took control of my life the day I decided to be the one behind the wheel, the day I stopped chasing and started leading the way."
John Maioran

Julie Fairhurst is the Founder of the Women Like Me Book Program. She is also a Certified Master Persuader, Sales Strategies, and Storyteller Coach. She started the Women Like Me Project to help women tell their stories. She helps her clients to share their message with the world through her unique storytelling programs. Julie has published 24 books and over 150 published authors to her credit.

Sales and marketing expert Julie helps women entrepreneurs build their influence and authority with their clients and customers so they can increase their revenue and profits. With a certification in persuasion and over 30 years of sales and marketing experience, Julie is an expert at understanding human behavior and what triggers people to make a purchase. She helps her clients develop marketing strategies that appeal to their target audience and provides coaching on how to close the sale.

In addition, she teaches her clients how to use the power of storytelling to engage and connect with their customers. As a result, they are able to build trust and credibility, which leads to more sales and higher conversion rates.

Julie is also a sought-after speaker, trainer, and prevention educator. She has been delivering empowering workshops to adolescents and adults on safety issues. She has presented to organizations such as the Vancouver Police Department, Justice Institute, University of British Columbia, and Capilano College. Behavioral Society of British Columbia, Surrey Memorial Hospital. Teachers Association of North Vancouver, and Shine Live, as well as appearing on television and in video.

When Julie was young, her home life was chaotic and tumultuous. Her parents were constantly fighting, and she felt unsafe and unloved. As a result, she developed some bad habits and made some poor decisions. As a teenager, she was headed down the wrong path, and it seemed like there was no hope for her.

But, somewhere deep inside, that little girl inside her showed up and reminded her that she wanted better for herself and her kids. Julie had no support from anyone, not a soul. She had to do it all on her own. She had no help from anyone, not a single person. She had to do everything by herself.

It's not easy to change your life. In fact, it can be downright difficult. But it's also necessary if you want to move forward. Sometimes, you must take a step backward before going forward. And that's what happened to Julie.

Julie is a woman who has achieved great success in her life despite facing many obstacles. She is a great example of someone who did not let anything stand in her way. Despite these challenges, she never gave up.

She went back to school and finished her education. She built an outstanding career in sales, marketing, and promotion. She won the company's top awards and was the first woman to achieve top sales-person year after year in a male-dominated industry. She was a sales manager for some of the country's most prestigious developers. She is an inspiration to everyone who knows her. She is proof that anything is possible with hard work and dedication.

Many people say that you should never look back, but Julie does.

Why? Because she wants to remember the journey that brought her to where she is today. And today, her life is very different.

Then, in 2019, Julie's beautiful 24-year-old niece died from a drug overdose on the streets of Vancouver, Canada. And that was the day she said enough! Her niece's death indirectly resulted from the generational beliefs and abuse that some of her siblings continue with their destructive lifestyles. So, when Julie says, "Enough is enough," she means it! Unfortunately, her story isn't unique.

When we don't face our issues, we pass on dysfunctional behaviors to future generations. This is what happened to my young niece.

This is why I started the Women Like Me organization. When children grow up in toxic environments, they often develop behavioral issues that follow them into adulthood. This can lead to serious problems in their relationships, careers, and mental health.

My young niece was a victim of this.

Everyone has a story, and everyone's story matters. No matter what you've been through, you can improve your life. It's not always easy, but with determination and perseverance, anything is possible.

The first step is to believe in yourself. You have the power to create whatever future you want for yourself.

The next step is to take action. You can't just sit and wait for good things to happen. You have to go out and make them happen. And finally, you have to persevere. There will be setbacks along the way, but that's no reason to give up. Keep going, and never give up on your dreams.

If you're willing to put in the work, you can change your life for the better. You have the power to do so. You just have to believe in yourself and take the steps to make it happen. So don't give up on yourself - you're capable of much more than you think. And when you're ready to get started, I'm here to help.

HERE IS HOW YOU CAN CONNECT WITH JULIE

Email: julie@changeyourpath.ca

Women Like Me Stories

www.womenlikemestories.com

Julie Fairhurst Academy

www.juliefairhurst.com

SOCIAL MEDIA

YouTube – Julie Fairhurst Women Like Me Stores and in Business

https://www.youtube.com/channel/UChFnLgiUC9mWnvp7jikKBw

Women Like Me on Facebook

https://www.facebook.com/StoryCoachJulieFairhurst

Julie Fairhurst Academy on Facebook

https://www.facebook.com/juliefairhurstcoaching

LinkedIn - Julie Fairhurst Certified Master Persuader

https://www.linkedin.com/in/salesstrategistjuliefairhurst/

Instagram – Women Like Me Stories

https://www.instagram.com/certified_master_persuader/

TikTok – Sales Strategist

https://www.tiktok.com/@juliethesalesstrategist

And soon my dear you will be able to fly …"

Samiha Totanj

Read More From Julie Fairhurst

Books are available on Amazon or the Women Like Me Stories website.

Sales and Personal Growth

Transferring Enthusiasm - The Sales Book For Your Business Growth

Positivity Makes All The Difference

Agent Etiquette – 14 Things You Didn't Learn in Real Estate School

7 Keys to Success – How to Become A Real Estate Badass

30 Days to Real Estate Action – Real Strategies & Real Connections

Why Agents Quit The Business

Powerful Persuasion – Unlocking the Five Key Strategies for Business Success

* * *

Women Like Me Book Series

Women Like Me – A Celebration of Courage and Triumphs

Women Like Me – Stories of Resilience and Courage

Women Like Me – A Tribute to the Brave and Wise

Women Like Me – Breaking Through the Silence

Women Like Me – From Loss to Living

Women Like Me – Healing and Acceptance

Women Like Me – Strong Women in Kenya

Women Like Me – Reclaiming Our Power

Women Like Me – Journey Through the Eyes of Kenya Women

Women Like Me – Whispers of Warriors: Women Who Refused to Stay Broken

* * *

Women Like Me Community Book Series

Women Like Me Community – Messages to My Younger Self

Women Like Me Community – Sharing Words of Gratitude

Women Like Me Community – Sharing What We Know to Be True

Women Like Me Community – Journal for Self-Discovery

Women Like Me Community – Sharing Life's Important Lessons

Women Like Me Community – Having Better Relationships

Women Like Me Community – Honoring The Women in Our Lives

Women Like Me Community – Letter's to our Future Selves

Manufactured by Amazon.ca
Acheson, AB